ENGLISH GRAMMAR
FOR
STUDENTS OF SPANISH

EMILY SPINELLI

UNIVERSITY OF MICHIGAN—DEARBORN

PREFACE BY DAVID L. WOLFE

The Olivia and Hill Press
P.O. Box 7396
Ann Arbor, Michigan 48107

English Grammar series
    edited by Jacqueline Morton

English Grammar for Students of French
English Grammar for Students of Spanish
English Grammar for Students of German
English Grammar for Students of Latin
English Grammar for Students of Italian
English Grammar for Students of Russian

Printed in the U.S.A.

First printing January 1980; second printing September 1980; third printing December 1981; fourth printing June 1984; fifth printing May 1985; sixth printing December 1985; seventh printing August 1987.

Library of Congress Catalog Card Number: 79-90976

ISBN 0-934034-01-X

< < Contents > >

<< Preface >>

English Grammar for Students of Spanish is a simple, practical, self-study manual written to aid high school and college students who are beginning the study of Spanish. It is patterned after the popular *English Grammar for Students of French* by Jacqueline Morton. It does not in any way replace the Spanish textbook, but is designed to supplement and enhance it. Both instructors and students will welcome the convenience and usefulness of this manual.

Students quickly discover that their Spanish textbook uses a variety of grammatical terms such as *verb conjugation, direct object pronoun, past participle,* or *present subjunctive.* Often students are unsure of the meanings and uses of such terminology and frequently they encounter terms which they have never heard before. This manual takes all the common grammatical terms that are necessary for learning to speak and write Spanish and (a) explains them clearly in English, (b) gives many English examples, and (c) shows the student step by step how to apply the concepts to Spanish. This is basic knowledge, explained simply, clearly, and in sufficient detail for maximum effectiveness. Although students can speak and write their native English without knowing how to identify parts of speech or the function of words, they must know these things in order to speak and write Spanish.

English Grammar for Students of Spanish assumes no knowledge of English grammar. It defines grammatical terms and concepts in a way particularly suited to students learning Spanish. Since the content and organization of the manual are based on a consensus of the material presented in beginning Spanish textbooks, it should help students (and their instructors) get the most out of the textbook they are using. It is designed to supplement any beginning text. In order to simplify the presentation, exceptions to Spanish grammatical rules as well as those points which have no English equivalents have been purposely omitted. Certain key Spanish and English structures have been singled out for a point-by-point comparison. For easy reference, there is a detailed word index.

Instructors may wish to make use in class of the many examples and contrastive analyses presented in the manual. Instructors whose students use the manual will not only save time preparing lessons, but will also save valuable class time which can be devoted to language practice.

Most Spanish instructors have long recognized the need for a handbook such as this. The simplicity, clarity, and thoroughness of the author's presentation make this manual eminently useful.

David L. Wolfe
University of Michigan

Ann Arbor
January 1980

< < Introduction > >

In order to learn a foreign language, in this case Spanish, you must look at every word in three ways: you must be aware of each word's meaning, class and use.

1. **Meaning** of the word. Each English word must be connected with a Spanish word which has an equivalent meaning.

> The English word *book* has the same meaning
> as the Spanish word **libro**.

Words with equivalent meanings must be learned by memorizing vocabulary items.

Sometimes two words are the same or very similar in both English and Spanish. These words are called **cognates** and are, of course, easy to learn.

Spanish	English
inteligente	intelligent
problema	problem
continuar	to continue

Occasionally knowing one Spanish word will help you learn another.

> Knowing that **niño** is *boy* should help you learn
> that **niña** is *girl*; or knowing that **hermano** is
> *brother* should help you remember that **hermana**
> is *sister*.

But generally there is little similarity between words and knowing one Spanish word will not help you learn another. Therefore, you must learn each vocabulary item separately.

> Knowing that *man* is **hombre** will not help you
> learn that *woman* is **mujer**.

1

In addition, sometimes words in combination will take on a special meaning.

> The Spanish word **hacer** means *to make*; **cola**
> means *tail*. However, **hacer cola** means *to line up*.

Such an expression whose meaning as a whole is different from the combination of individual words is called an **idiom**. You will need to pay special attention to idioms in order to recognize them and use them correctly.

2. **Class** of a word. English and Spanish words are grouped according to class, i.e., **part of speech**. There are eight different parts of speech:

> | | |
> |---|---|
> | noun | article |
> | verb | adverb |
> | pronoun | preposition |
> | adjective | conjunction |

Each part of speech has its own rules for spelling, pronunciation and use. You must learn to identify the part of speech to which a word belongs in order to choose the correct Spanish equivalent and know what rules for spelling apply.

Look at the word *that* in the following sentences:

> a. *That* girl is my sister.
> b. There is the car *that* he bought.
> c. We didn't talk about *that*.

The English word is the same in all three sentences, but in Spanish three different words will be used because each *that* belongs to a different part of speech.[1]

3. **Use** of a word. In addition to its class as a part of speech each word has a special **function** or use within a sentence. A noun, for example, can be used as a subject, direct object, indirect

---

[1] a. Demonstrative adjective – see p. 89.
  b. Relative pronoun – see p. 135.
  c. Demonstrative pronoun – see p. 125.

object, or object of a preposition. Determining the function of the word will help you choose the correct Spanish equivalent and know what rules apply.

Look at the word **him** in the following sentences:

    a. They don't see *him*.
    b. I wrote *him* a letter.
    c. Are you going with *him*?

In English the word is the same but the Spanish equivalent will be different in each sentence because the pronoun *him* has three different uses.[1]

NOTE: As a student of Spanish you must learn to recognize both parts of speech and the use of words within a sentence. This is essential because in Spanish words have a great deal of influence upon each other.

Compare the following sentence in English and Spanish.

The small red shoes are on the heavy round table.

Los pequeños zapatos rojos están sobre la pesada mesa redonda.

In English: The only word that affects another word in the sentence is *shoes*, which affects *are*. If the word were *shoe*, *are* would be *is*.

In Spanish: The word for *shoes* (**zapatos**) not only affects *are* (**están**) but also the spelling and pronunciation of the equivalent words for *the, small*, and *red*.

    The word for *table* (**mesa**) affects the spelling and pronunciation of the equivalent words for *the, heavy*, and *round*.

    The only word which is not affected by the words surrounding it is **sobre**, meaning *on*.

---

[1] a. Direct object — see p. 103.
  b. Indirect object — see p. 103.
  c. Object of a preposition — see p. 107.

Since parts of speech and function are usually determined in the same way in English and Spanish, this handbook will show you how to identify them in English. You will then learn to compare English and Spanish constructions. This will give you a better understanding of the grammar explanations in your Spanish textbook.

< < What is a Noun? > >

A **noun** is a word that can be the name of:

- a person   teacher, husband, girl, Mr. Smith, Tom, Karen

- a place   state, continent, Madrid, Spain, Mt. Everest, Niagara Falls

- a thing or animal   map, boat, sea, fish, dog, cow

- an idea   love, hate, greed, democracy

Nouns that always begin with a capital letter, such as the names of people and places (John Smith, Spain), are called **proper nouns**. Nouns that do not begin with a capital letter (dog, love, girl) are called **common nouns**.

To help you learn to recognize nouns, here is a paragraph where the nouns are in italics:

The *countries* which make up the Hispanic-speaking *world* export *products* which we use every *day*. *Spain* produces many of the *shoes, purses, gloves* and other leather[1] *articles* sold in the *United States*. *Spain* also sells us much *wine* and *sherry*. The *islands* of the *Caribbean* and the *nations* of *Central America* supply us with tropical *fruits* such as *bananas* and *papayas*; *sugar* is another important *export* of these *regions*. *Coffee* and *chocolate* are grown in several *countries* of *Latin America*. The petroleum[1] *products* of *Mexico* and *Venezuela* are a major *source* of *income* for their national *economies*.

---

[1]These are examples of a noun used as an adjective, that is, to describe another noun. See p. 80.

< < What is Meant by Gender? > >

When a word can be classified as to whether it is **masculine, feminine,** or **neuter,** it is said to have a **gender.**

Gender plays a very small role in English; however, since it is at the very heart of the Spanish language, let us see what evidence of gender we have in English.

In English: When we use a noun we often do not realize that it has a gender. But when we replace the noun with *he, she,* or *it,* we choose only one of the three without hesitation because we automatically give a gender to the noun we are replacing. The gender corresponds to the sex of the person we are replacing.

> The *boy* came home; *he* was tired and I was glad to see *him*.

>> A noun (*boy*) is of the **masculine gender** if *he* or *him* is used to substitute for it.

> My *aunt* came for a visit; *she* is nice and I like *her*.

>> A noun (*aunt*) is of the **feminine gender** if *she* or *her* is used to substitute for it.

> There is a *tree* in front of the house. *It* is a maple.

>> A noun (*tree*) is of the **neuter gender** if *it* is substituted for it.[1]

In Spanish: All nouns, common nouns and proper nouns, are either masculine or feminine. There is no such thing as a neuter noun. This means that all objects, animals, and abstract ideas have a gender, as have the names of countries.

---

[1] There are a few well-known exceptions, such as *ship*, which is referred to as *she*. It is custom, not logic, which decides.

The S/S United States sailed for Europe. She is a beautiful ship.

Unlike English, where the few examples of gender are based on the sex of the noun, gender in Spanish cannot be explained or figured out. It is a question of the Spanish language itself.

Examples of English nouns whose equivalents are *masculine* in Spanish:	Examples of English nouns whose equivalents are *feminine* in Spanish:
money	coin
book	library
country	nation
Peru	Argentina
heaven	war
Wednesday	peace
sorrow	health
problem	philosophy

You will have to memorize each noun with its gender. This gender is important not only for the noun itself, but for the spelling and pronunciation of the words it influences.

Gender can sometimes be determined by looking at the ending of a noun. Below are some noun endings which often correspond to the masculine gender and others which correspond to the feminine gender. Since you will encounter many nouns with these endings in your Spanish course, you should familiarize yourself with them.[1]

Feminine Endings

-a	la casa, la biblioteca	*house, library*
-d	la edad, la ciudad	*age, city*
-z	la nariz	*nose*
-ción	la educación, la nación	*education, nation*
-umbre	la costumbre	*custom*
-ie	la especie	*species*

[1] This table of endings has been adapted from John J. Bergen. "A Simplified Approach for Teaching the Gender of Spanish Nouns." *Hispania*, LXI (December, 1978), 875.

Masculine Endings

Any ending except those given above.

In particular:

-l	el papel	*paper*
-o	el libro	*book*
-n	el jardín	*garden*
-e	el parque	*park*
-r	el dolor	*pain*
-s	el interés	*interest*

To help you remember these endings note that for the masculine endings the letters spell "loners."

There are of course many exceptions to the above rules: **la mano** (*the hand*) is one common exception. Your textbook and instructor will point out the exceptions which you will have to learn individually.

< < What is Meant by Number? > >

When a word refers to one person or thing, it is said to be **singular**; when it refers to more than one, it is called **plural**.

Some nouns, called **collective nouns**, refer to a group of persons or things, but they are considered singular.

A football *team* has eleven players.
The *family* is well.
The *crowd* was under control.

In English: We indicate the plural of nouns in several ways:

- by adding an *-s* or *-es* to a singular noun

    book → book*s*
    kiss → kiss*es*

- sometimes by making a spelling change

    m*an* → m*en*
    lea*f* → lea*ves*

A plural noun is usually spelled differently and sounds different from the singular.

In Spanish: A word in the plural is spelled and pronounced differently from its singular form. Nouns or adjectives which end

- in a vowel add -s to form a plural:

    casa → casas   *house → houses*
    libro → libros   *book → books*

- in a consonant add -es to form a plural:

    papel → papeles   *paper → papers*
    dolor → dolores   *pain → pains*

A few nouns will have internal spelling changes when they become plural. One such common change is -z to -c: lápiz → lápices (*pencil → pencils*). Your textbook will point out other exceptions to the two basic rules listed above.

NOTE: Nouns do not change gender when they become plural.

< < **What are Indefinite and Definite Articles?** > >

The **article** is a word which is placed before a noun to show if the noun refers to a particular person, thing, animal or object or if the noun refers to an unspecified person, thing, animal or object.

In English: A. Indefinite Articles

A or *an* is used before a noun when we do not speak of a particular person, thing, animal or object. They are called indefinite articles.

I saw *a* boy in the street.
  not a particular boy

I ate *an* apple.
  not a particular apple

The indefinite articles *a*, *an* are used with a singular noun. If the noun becomes plural, the indefinite article is omitted or replaced by the word *some*.

I saw boys in the street.
I saw *some* boys in the street.

I ate apples.
I ate *some* apples.

B. Definite Articles

The is used before a noun when we are speaking of a particular person, thing, animal or object. It is called the definite article.

I saw *the* boy you spoke to me about.
  a particular boy

I ate *the* apple you gave me.
  a particular apple

The definite article remains *the* when the noun becomes plural.

I saw *the boys* you spoke to me about.

I ate *the apples* you gave me.

In Spanish: The article, definite or indefinite, has a much greater role than its English equivalent. It works hand in hand with the noun it belongs to in that it matches the noun's gender and number. This "matching" is called **agreement**. (One says that "the article agrees with the noun.") You use a different article depending on whether the noun is masculine or feminine, and depending on whether the noun is singular or plural.

A. **Indefinite articles** precede the noun they accompany.

- **un** indicates a masculine singular noun

    un libro   *a book*
    un muchacho   *a boy*

- **una** indicates a feminine singular noun

    una casa   *a house*
    una muchacha   *a girl*

- **unos** indicates a masculine plural noun

    unos libros   *some books*
    unos muchachos   *some boys*

- **unas** indicates a feminine plural noun

    unas casas   *some houses*
    unas muchachas   *some girls*

B. **Definite articles** precede the noun they accompany.

- **el** indicates a masculine singular noun

    el libro   *the book*
    el muchacho   *the boy*

- **la** indicates a feminine singular noun

    la casa   *the house*
    la muchacha   *the girl*

- **los** indicates a masculine plural noun

los libros	*the books*
los muchachos	*the boys*

- **las** indicates a feminine plural noun

las casas	*the houses*
las muchachas	*the girls*

Memorize nouns with their singular definite article; the article will tell you if the noun is masculine or feminine.[1]

The definite article is used much more frequently in Spanish than in English.

La guerra es terrible.
War   is terrible.

Esa mujer es **la** señora Gómez.
That lady is   Mrs. Gómez.

Your textbook will instruct you on the uses of the definite and indefinite article.

< < What is the Possessive? > >

The term **possessive** means that one noun *possesses* or owns another noun.

In English: You can show possession in one of two ways:

---

[1] There are only a few exceptions to this statement. The primary exceptions are those feminine nouns that begin with a stressed **a-** and which for pronunciation purposes take **el** as the article: **el agua, el águila.** The noun is nonetheless still feminine: **el agua fría.**

1. With an **apostrophe**

   - by adding **apostrophe + s** to a singular possessor

     John*'s* shirt
     the girl*'s* dress
     the boy*'s* shirt

   - by adding an **apostrophe** to a plural possessor

     the girl*s'* father
     the boy*s'* team

2. With the word *of*

   - by adding *of* before a singular proper name

     the shirt *of* John

   - by adding *of the* before other noun possessors

     the dress *of the* girl
     the shirt *of the* boy
     the father *of the* girls
     the team *of the* boys

In Spanish: There is only one way to express possession and that is by using *of* (de). The apostrophe structure does not exist. When you want to show possession in Spanish you must change a structure using an apostrophe to a structure using *of* (de).

John*'s* shirt	→	*the shirt of John* la camisa de Juan
the girl*'s* dress	→	*the dress of the girl* el vestido **de la** muchacha
the boy*'s* shirt	→	*the shirt of the boy* la camisa **del** muchacho
		de + el → del
the girl*s'* father	→	*the father of the girls* el padre **de las** muchachas
the boy*s'* team	→	*the team of the boys* el equipo **de los** muchachos

< < What is a Verb? > >

A **verb** is a word that indicates an action, mental state or condition. The action can be physical, as in such verbs as *run, walk, hit, sit,* or mental, as in such verbs as *dream, think, believe,* and *hope.*

The verb is one of the most important words of a sentence, and you cannot express a complete thought (i.e., write a **complete sentence**) without a verb.

To help you learn to recognize verbs, here is a paragraph where the verbs are in italics:

> The three students *entered* the restaurant, *selected* a table, *hung* up their coats and *sat* down. They *looked* at the menu and *asked* the waitress what she *recommended*. She *advised* the daily special, beef stew. It *was* not expensive. They *chose* a bottle of red wine and *ordered* a salad. The service *was* slow, but the food *tasted* excellent. Good cooking, they *decided, takes* time. They *ordered* pastry for dessert and *finished* the meal with coffee.

A **transitive verb** is a verb which can take a direct object. (See **What are Objects?**, p. 102.) It is indicated by a (*v.t.*) in the dictionary.

The boy *threw* the ball.   to throw—transitive verb
                 /
          direct object

She *quit* her job.   to quit—transitive verb
              /
       direct object

An **intransitive verb** is a verb that does not take a direct object. It is indicated by (*v.i.*) in the dictionary.

Paul *is sleeping.*   to sleep—intransitive verb

She *arrives* today.   to arrive—intransitive verb
              /
         adverb

Many verbs can be used transitively or intransitively, depending on whether they have a direct object in the sentence or not.

The students *speak* French.   to speak—transitive verb

direct object

Actions *speak* louder than words.

adverb   to speak—intransitive verb

In English: It is possible to change the meaning of a verb by placing little words (*prepositions* or *adverbs*) after them (Column A):

Column A	Column B
to look *for* I am looking for a book.	to search for
to look *after* I look after children.	to take care of
to look *out* Look out for lions.	to beware of
to look *into* He will look into it.	to investigate
to look *over* Look over the exam.	to check

In Spanish: You cannot change the meaning of a verb by adding these little words. In Spanish you would have to use an entirely different verb in each of the above sentences.

When looking up verbs in the dictionary, be sure to look up the specific meaning of the verb (Column B).

< < What is an Infinitive? > >

An **infinitive** is a form of the verb. It can be considered the name of the verb; it is the form of the verb found in the dictionary as the main entry. The infinitive can never be used as the main verb of a sentence; there must always be another verb with it.

In English: The infinitive is composed of two words, *to* + **verb**: *to walk, to think, to be, to listen.* The infinitive is always used with a conjugated verb. (See **What is a Verb Conjugation?**, p. 29.)

> John and Mary *want to dance* together.
>   main verb   infinitive

> It *started to rain.*
>   main verb   infinitive

> *To learn is* exciting.
>   infinitive   main verb

> It*'s* (*it is*) important *to be* on time.
>   main verb   infinitive

In Spanish: The infinitive is composed of only one word which ends with the letters **-ar, -er,** or **-ir**.

hablar	*to speak*
comer	*to eat*
vivir	*to live*

You could say that the infinitive endings (**-ar, -er, -ir**) mean "to" in English while the beginning letters of the infinitive carry the meaning of the word.

In the case of the infinitive **cantar**

> cantar   *to sing*
> sing to

In a sentence the infinitive form is always used for a verb that depends upon another verb which is not an auxiliary verb. (See **What are Auxiliary Verbs?**, p. 18.)

*John and Mary want **to dance** together.*
Juan y María quieren **bailar** juntos.
infinitive

*It started **to rain**.*
Empezó a **llover**.
infinitive

*I can **swim**.*
Puedo **nadar**.
infinitive

*You should **study** more.*
Usted debe **estudiar** más.
infinitive

Notice that in the last two examples there is no "to" in the English sentence to alert you that in Spanish an infinitive must be used.

NOTES:

< < What are Auxiliary Verbs? > >

Some verbs can also be **auxiliary verbs** (also known as **helping verbs**); these auxiliary verbs help the main verb express an action or make a statement.

Mary *is* a girl.	*is*	main verb
Paul *has* a headache.	*has*	main verb
They *go* to the movies.	*go*	main verb
They ***have gone*** to the movies.	***have***	auxiliary verb
	gone	main verb
His wife ***has been*** *gone* for two months.	***has***	auxiliary verb
	been	auxiliary verb
	gone	main verb

In English: There are many auxiliary verbs. They have two main uses:

1. to help formulate questions

Bob *has* a dog.	*has*	main verb
Does Bob *have* a dog?	***does***	auxiliary verb
	have	main verb
They *talked* on the phone.	*talked*	main verb
Did they *talk* on the phone?	***did***	auxiliary verb
	talk	main verb

2. to indicate the tense of the main verb (present, future, past— see **What is Meant by Tense?**, p. 43.)

Mary *is* reading a book.	Present
Mary *was* reading a book.	Past
Mary *will* read a book.	Future

In Spanish: There are three verbs which can be used as auxiliary verbs: **haber, estar** and **ser**.

1. **haber** as an auxiliary is used to form the many perfect tenses. (See **What are the Perfect Tenses?**, p. 59.)

El hombre **ha comido** demasiado.
       auxiliary   main verb
        haber

*The man **has eaten** too much.*

Los estudiantes ya **habían llegado**.
         auxiliary   main verb
         haber

*The students **had already arrived**.*

2. **estar** as an auxiliary is used to form the progressive tenses. (See **What is a Progressive Tense?**, p. 50.)

Estoy leyendo un libro ahora.
auxiliary   main verb
  estar

I am reading a book now.

Estábamos escuchando la radio.
 auxiliary   main verb
  estar

*We **were listening** to the radio.*

3. **ser** as an auxiliary verb is used to form the true passive voice. (See **What is Meant by Active and Passive Voice?**, p. 76.)

El puente **fue construido** por los romanos.
      auxiliary main verb
     ser

*The bridge **was constructed** by the Romans.*

Since the other English auxiliary verbs such as *do, does, did, will* or *would* do not exist as separate words in Spanish, you cannot translate them as such. In Spanish the meaning conveyed by these auxiliary verbs is indicated by the last letters, i.e., the ending, of the main verb. You will find more on this subject under the different tenses.

< < What is a Subject? > >

In a sentence the person or thing that performs the action is called the **subject**. When you wish to find the subject of a sentence, always look for the verb first; then ask, *who?* or *what?* **before the verb.** The answer will be the subject.

John speaks French.

Who speaks French?   Answer: John.
John is the subject.   (Singular subject)

Are John and Mary coming tonight?

Who is coming tonight?   Answer: John and Mary.
John and Mary is the subject. (Plural subject)

Train yourself to always ask the question to find the subject. Never assume a word is the subject because it comes first in the sentence. Subjects can be in many different places of a sentence as you can see in the following examples in which the *subject* is in boldface and the *verb* italicised:

Did the **game** *start* on time?
After playing for two hours, ***John*** *became* exhausted.
Looking in the mirror *was* a little **girl**.

Some sentences have more than one main verb; you have to find the subject of each verb.

The ***boys*** *were doing* the cooking while ***Mary*** *was setting* the table.

Boys is the plural subject of *were doing*.
Mary is the singular subject of *was setting*.

In English and in Spanish it is very important to find the subject of each verb and to make sure that the subject and verb agree. You must choose the form of the verb which goes with the subject: if the subject is singular, the verb must be singular; if the subject is plural, the verb must be plural. (See **What is a Verb Conjugation?**, p. 29.)

< < What is a Pronoun? > >

A **pronoun** is a word used in place of one or more nouns. It may stand, therefore, for a person, place, thing or idea.

For instance, instead of repeating the proper noun "Paul" in the following two sentences, we would use a pronoun in the second sentence:

Paul likes to sing. *Paul* goes to practice every day.

Paul likes to sing. *He* goes to practice every day.

A pronoun can only be used to refer to something (or someone) that has already been mentioned. The word that the pronoun replaces is called the **antecedent** of the pronoun.

In the example above, the pronoun *he* refers to the proper noun *Paul. Paul* is the antecedent of the pronoun *he.*

In English: There are different types of pronouns. They are studied in separate sections of this handbook. Below we will simply list the most important categories and refer you to the section where they are discussed in detail.

Pronouns change in form in the different persons and according to the function they have in the sentence.

- **Subject pronouns** (see p. 23)

    I go. *They* read. *He* runs.

- **Direct object pronouns** (see p. 110)

    Paul loves *her*.

    Jane saw *them* at the theater.

- **Indirect object pronouns** (see p. 110)

    The boy wrote *me* the letter.

    John gave *us* the book.

- **Object of preposition pronouns** (see p. 114)

    Robert is going to the movies with *us*.

    Don't step on *it*; walk around *it*.

- **Reflexive pronouns** — These pronouns are used with reflexive verbs (see p. 74).

    I cut *myself*. We washed *ourselves*.

- **Interrogative pronouns** — These pronouns are used in questions (see p. 120).

    Who is that? *What* do you want?

- **Demonstrative pronouns** — These pronouns are used to point out persons or things (see p. 125).

    This (one) is expensive. *That* (one) is cheap.

- **Possessive pronouns** — These pronouns are used to show possession (see p. 129).

    Whose book is that? *Mine. Yours* is on the table.

- **Relative pronouns** — These pronouns are used to introduce relative subordinate clauses (see p. 135).

    The man *who* came is very nice.
    Mary *whom* you met is the president of the company.

In Spanish: Pronouns are identified in the same way as in English. The most important difference is that a pronoun agrees with the noun it replaces; that is, it must correspond in gender (and usually in number) with its antecedent.

< < What is a Subject Pronoun? > >

A **subject pronoun** is a pronoun used as a subject of a verb:

He ran but *I* walked.

> Who ran? Answer: He.
> *He* is the subject of the verb *ran*.

> Who walked? Answer: I.
> *I* is the subject of the verb *walked*.

Let us compare the subject pronouns of English and Spanish. The subject pronouns are divided into six groups according to the person speaking (the **first person**), the person spoken to (the **second person**), or the person spoken about (the **third person**). These groups are further divided according to singular or plural.

English		Spanish
I	1st person singular the person speaking	**yo**
you	2nd person singular the person spoken to	**tú**
he *she* *it*	3rd person singular person or thing spoken about by 1st and 2nd persons	**él** **ella** **usted** [you]
we	1st person plural the person speaking plus others *John and I* speak Spanish. we	**nosotros** **nosotras**
you	2nd person plural the persons spoken to	**vosotros** **vosotras**
they	3rd person plural the persons or things spoken about by the 1st and 2nd persons	**ellos** **ellas** **ustedes** [you]

As you can see there are several words for "you" in Spanish. **Tú, vosotros/vosotras** are 2nd person pronouns; they are called **familiar** *you*. **Usted** and **ustedes** are 3rd person pronouns and are called **formal** *you*. To help you learn how to choose the correct form of *you* in Spanish an entire section has been devoted to **"What is Meant by Familiar and Formal You?"**

< < What is Meant by Familiar and Formal You? > >

In English: There is no difference between "you" in the singular and "you" in the plural. If you were in a room with many people and asked aloud "Are *you* coming with me?" the "you" could refer to one person or many; it could also refer to close friends or complete strangers.

In Spanish: There is a difference between "you" in the singular and "you" in the plural; there is also a difference between the "you" used with close friends, the **familiar** *you*, and the "you" used with persons you do not know well, the **formal** *you.*

- **Familiar** *you*

    The familiar forms of *you* are used with members of one's family, friends, children and pets. In general, you use the familiar forms with persons you call by a first name.

    tú   familiar singular *you*.
                    It can refer to a male or female.

        Juan, ¿cómo estás **tú**?
        John, how are **you**?

        María, ¿cómo estás **tú**?
        Mary, how are **you**?

vosotros   familiar plural *you*, masculine form.
It can refer to all males or a group of males and females.

Juan y Pablo, ¿cómo estáis **vosotros**?
John and Paul, how are you?

Juan y María, ¿cómo estáis **vosotros**?
John and Mary, how are you?

vosotras   familiar plural *you*, feminine form.
It refers to all females.

María y Ana, ¿cómo estáis **vosotras**?
Mary and Ann, how are you?

Note: The plural familiar forms **vosotros** and **vosotras** are used only in Spain. In Latin America **ustedes** is used as the plural of **tú**. See below.

- **Formal** *you*

The formal forms of *you* are used to address persons you do not know well or persons to whom you should show respect. In general, you use the formal forms with persons you address with a title: Ms. Smith, Mr. Jones, Dr. Anderson, Professor Gómez.

usted   formal singular *you*.
It can refer to a male or female.

Señor Gómez, ¿cómo está **usted**?
Mr. Gómez, how are you?

Señora Gómez, ¿cómo está **usted**?
Mrs. Gómez, how are you?

ustedes   formal plural *you*.
It can refer to both males and females.

Professor Gómez y Doctor García, ¿cómo están **ustedes**?
Professor Gómez and Dr. García, how are you?

Note: In Latin America **ustedes** is the plural of both the familiar and formal forms; **vosotros/vosotras** are not used.

In Latin America **ustedes** would be used in the following situations:

Professor Gómez y Doctor García, ¿cómo están **ustedes**?
Professor Gómez and Dr. García, how are you?

Juan y Pablo, ¿cómo están **ustedes**?
John and Paul, how are you?

Ana y María, ¿cómo están **ustedes**?
Ann and Mary, how are you?

Here is a table you can use as reference:

		English	Spanish	
			Spain	Latin America
Familiar	**Singular**	you	tú	tú
	Plural	you	vosotros vosotras	ustedes
Formal	**Singular**	you	usted	usted
	Plural	you	ustedes	ustedes

If you are in doubt as to whether to use the familiar or formal forms, use the formal forms unless speaking to a child or animal. The formal forms of *you* show respect for the person you are talking to and use of familiar forms can be considered rude if you do not know a person well.

In order to choose the correct form of *you* in Spanish, you should ask yourself the following questions:

1. Do you need the familiar or formal form?

2. If you need the formal form:

    • Are you speaking to one person?
       Then the form is singular.   **usted**

    • Are you speaking to more than one person?
       Then the form is plural.   **ustedes**

3. If you need the familiar form:

- Are you speaking to one person?
  Then the form is singular.   **tú**

- Are you speaking to more than one person?
  Then the form is plural, but the plural form you
  will choose depends on the country you are in.

- Are you in Latin America?
  Then the form is the same as the formal
  plural form.   **ustedes**

  Are you in Spain?
  Then the form will depend on the gender (sex)
  of the group you are addressing.

    Are you speaking to a group of all males or
    males and females?
    Then the form is masculine.   **vosotros**

    Are you speaking to a group of all females?
    Then the form is feminine.   **vosotras**

Let's find the Spanish equivalent for *you* in the following
sentences.

- *Mr. President, are **you** coming with us?*

    Do you need familiar or formal forms? Formal.
    Is the you singular or plural? Singular.
    Then the form is **usted.**

  Señor Presidente, ¿viene **usted** con nosotros?

- *Mr. and Mrs. Lado, are **you** coming with us?*

    Do you need familiar or formal forms? Formal.
    Is the you singular or plural? Plural.
    Then the form is **ustedes.**

  Señor y señora Lado, ¿vienen **ustedes** con nosotros?

- *John, are **you** coming with us*?

  Do you need familiar or formal forms? Familiar.
  Is the you singular or plural? Singular
  Then the form is **tú**.

Juan, ¿vienes **tú** con nosotros?

- *Isabel and Gloria, are **you** coming with us*?

  Do you need familiar or formal forms?   Familiar.
  Is the you singular or plural?   Plural.
  Are you in Spain or Latin America?   Spain.
  Does the you refer to a mixed or all male group or to a
    group of females?   Females.
  Then the form is **vosotras**.

Isabel y Gloria, ¿venís **vosotras** con nosotros?

- *Vincent and John, are **you** coming with us?*

  Do you need familiar or formal forms?   Familiar.
  Is the you singular or plural?   Plural.
  Are you in Spain or Latin America?   Latin America.
  Then the form is **ustedes**.

Vicente y Juan, ¿vienen **ustedes** con nosotros?

NOTES:

< < What is a Verb Conjugation? > >

A **verb conjugation** is a list of the six possible forms of the verb for a particular tense; there is one verb form for each of the six persons used as the subject of the verb. (See **What is a Subject Pronoun?**, p. 23.)

In English: Most verbs change very little. Let us look at the various forms of the verb *to sing* when each of the possible pronouns is the performer of the action.

1st per. sing.	*I sing* with the music.
2nd per. sing.	*You sing* with the music.
3rd per. sing.	*He sings* with the music.
	She sings with the music.
	It sings with the music.
1st per. pl.	*We sing* with the music.
2nd per. pl.	*You sing* with the music.
3rd per. pl.	*They sing* with the music.

There is only one change in the verb forms; in the 3rd person singular the verb adds an "-s." Conjugating verbs in English is relatively easy since there are only two forms. This is definitely not the case in Spanish.

In Spanish: Each verb has six different forms. It is necessary to memorize the form of the verb which corresponds to each of the six persons. Memorizing six forms for all verbs that exist would be an impossible and endless task. Fortunately, Spanish verbs are divided into two overall categories:

1. **Regular verbs** — Verbs whose forms follow a regular pattern; only one sample must be memorized and the pattern can then be applied to all other verbs in the same group.

2. **Irregular verbs** — Verbs whose forms do not follow any regular pattern and must be memorized individually.

A. Let us now conjugate in Spanish the verb *to sing* which we conjugated before in English. Pay special attention to the subject.

1st per. sing.	**yo** canto
2nd per. sing.	**tú** cantas
3rd per. sing.	{ **él** canta **ella** canta **usted** canta
1st per. pl.	**nosotros** cantamos **nosotras** cantamos
2nd per. pl.	**vosotros** cantáis **vosotras** cantáis
3rd per. sing.	{ **ellos** cantan **ellas** cantan **ustedes** cantan

Let us examine the six persons of the verb conjugation and the possible subjects which belong to each person.

- **1st person singular**—The *I form* of the verb is used whenever the person speaking is the doer of the action.

   Yo canto mucho.
   I sing a lot.

   Generalmente **yo canto** muy bien.
   Normally, I sing very well.

   Notice that **yo** is not capitalized except as the first word of a sentence.

- **2nd person singular**—The *you familiar singular form* of the verb (the **tú** form) is used whenever the person spoken to (with whom you are on familiar terms) is the doer of the action.

   Juan, **tú cantas** muy bien.
   John, you sing very well.

   María, **tú cantas** muy bien.
   Mary, you sing very well.

- **3rd person singular**—The *3rd person singular form* (the él form) of the verb is used with many possible subjects.

1. the third person singular masculine pronoun él (*he, it*) and the third person singular feminine pronoun ella (*she, it*):

    El **canta** muy bien.
    *He **sings** very well.*

    Ella **canta** muy bien.
    *She **sings** very well.*

2. The singular pronoun usted (*you*):

    Señor Gómez, **usted canta** muy bien.
    *Mr. Gómez, **you sing** very well.*

    Señorita Gómez, **usted canta** muy bien.
    *Miss Gómez, **you sing** very well.*

3. One proper name:

    María **canta** muy bien.
    *Mary **sings** very well.*

    Pedro **canta** muy bien.
    *Peter **sings** very well.*

    El señor García **canta** muy bien.
    *Mr. García **sings** very well.*

4. A singular noun:

    El hombre **canta** muy bien.
    *The man **sings** very well.*

    La niña **canta** muy bien.
    *The girl **sings** very well.*

    El pájaro **canta** muy bien.
    *The bird **sings** very well.*

- **1st person plural**—The *we form* (**nosotros** form) of the verb is used whenever "I" (the speaker) is one of the doers of the action; that is, whenever the speaker is included in a plural or multiple subject.

  The students and I sing very well.

  In Spanish: **nosotros** verb form

  Los estudiantes y yo **cantamos** muy bien.

  Isabel, Gloria and I sing very well.

  In Spanish: **nosotros** verb form

  Isabel, Gloria y yo **cantamos** muy bien.

In the two sentences above the subject could be replaced by the pronoun *we*, so that in Spanish you must use the **nosotros** form (1st person plural) of the verb.

- **2nd person plural**—The *you familiar plural form* of the verb (**vosotros** form) is used only in Spain when you are addressing two or more persons with whom you would use **tú** individually.

  John and you sing very well.

  In Spanish: **vosotros** verb form

  Juan y tú **cantáis** muy bien.

  Mary, Susan and you sing very well.

  In Spanish: **vosotros** verb form

  María, Susana y tú **cantáis** muy bien.

In the two sentences above you say **tú** to each person individually so the subjects could be replaced by the familiar plural *you*: **vosotros/vosotras**. In Spanish you must use the **vosotros** (second person plural) form of the verb in the above sentences.

- **3rd person plural**—The *they form* of the verb (**ellos** form) is used with many possible subjects.

  1. the third person plural masculine pronoun **ellos** (*they*) and the third person plural feminine pronoun **ellas** (*they*):

     Ellos cantan muy bien.
     They sing very well.

     Ellas cantan muy bien.
     They sing very well.

  2. the plural pronoun **ustedes** (*you*):

     Señor y señora García, **ustedes cantan** muy bien.
     Mr. and Mrs. García, you sing very well.

  3. two or more names:

     Isabel, Gloria and Robert sing very well.
                In Spanish: **ellos** verb form

     Isabel, Gloria y Roberto **cantan** muy bien.

     Mrs. Gómez and Mrs. Jiménez sing very well.
                In Spanish: **ellos** verb form

     La señora Gómez y la señora Jiménez **cantan** muy bien.

  4. two or more singular nouns:

     The girl and her father sing very well.
                In Spanish: **ellos** verb form

     La chica y su padre **cantan** muy bien.

  5. a plural noun:

     The girls sing very well.
       In Spanish: **ellos** verb form

     Las chicas **cantan** muy bien.

B. Let us again look at the conjugation of the same verb *to sing* paying special attention to the verb forms. Notice that each of the six persons has a different verb form. However, when several pronouns belong to the same person there is only one verb form. The 3rd person singular has three pronouns: **él, ella** and **usted** but they all have the same verb form: **canta**.

yo	can**to**
tú	can**tas**
él ella usted	can**ta**
nosotros nosotras	can**tamos**
vosotros vosotras	can**táis**
ellos ellas ustedes	can**tan**

The Spanish verb is composed of two parts:

1. The **stem** (also called *the root*) which is found by dropping the last two letters from the infinitive.

Infinitive	Stem
can**tar**	cant-
co**mer**	com-
vi**vir**	viv-

The stem will usually not change throughout a conjugation. In certain verbs, however, the stem will change in a minor way; such verbs are called **stem-changing verbs**.

2. The **ending** which changes for each person in the conjugation of regular and irregular verbs.

Spanish verbs are divided into three groups, also called **conjugations**, based on the infinitive ending. Unlike English where the infinitive is the word "to" plus a verb, in Spanish the infinitive form is a special ending attached to the stem (see p. 16). The three endings are:

-ar	-er	-ir
1st conjugation	2nd conjugation	3rd conjugation

Each of the three verb conjugations has its own set of verb endings. You will have to memorize only one sample verb for each conjugation in order to conjugate any regular verb which belongs to that group. As an example, let's look more closely at regular verbs of the first conjugation, that is, verbs like **cantar** (*to sing*), **hablar** (*to speak*), or **tomar** (*to take*) which have the same infinitive ending -**ar**.

Subject	Ending
yo	-o
tú	-as
él ella usted	-a
nosotros nosotras	-amos
vosotros vosotras	-áis
ellos ellas ustedes	-an

After you have memorized the endings for a verb like **cantar**, you can then conjugate any regular -ar verb. Let's conjugate the verbs **hablar** and **tomar**.

1. Identify the conjugation of the verb by its infinitive ending:

   -**ar** or first conjugation

2. Find the verb stem:

   hablar → habl-   tomar → tom-

3. Add the ending that agrees with the subject.

Subject	Verb form	Verb form
yo	hablo	tomo
tú	hablas	tomas
él ella usted	habla	toma
nosotros nosotras	hablamos	tomamos
vosotros vosotras	habláis	tomáis
ellos ellas ustedes	hablan	toman

The endings for -er and -ir verbs will be different, but the process of conjugation is always the same for regular verbs:

1. Identify the conjugation of the verb by its infinitive ending.

2. Find the verb stem.

3. According to the conjugation, add the ending that agrees with the subject.

As you can see, in Spanish the verb ending indicates the subject. For instance, **hablo** can only have **yo** as a subject. Similarly, the subject of **hablas** can only be **tú**; the subject of **hablamos**, **nosotros**; the subject of **habláis**, **vosotros**.

Since you know the subject from the verb form, the subject pronoun is often omitted.

I speak	hablo
you speak	hablas
we speak	hablamos
you speak	habláis

If you do include the subject pronoun it adds strong emphasis to the subject:

yo canto
I sing (but he doesn't)

nosotros cantamos
we sing (but they don't)

However, in the third person singular and plural it is often necessary to include the pronoun in order to avoid any doubt about who is the subject of the verb.

habla *could be*	él habla	*he speaks*
	ella habla	*she speaks*
	usted habla	*you speak*
hablan *could be*	ellos hablan	*they speak*
	ellas hablan	*they speak*
	ustedes hablan	*you speak*

The subject pronouns are included to clear up or clarify who the subject is in the above examples.

NOTE: Subject pronouns are used far less frequently in Spanish than in English. You use them only to add emphasis or to clarify the subject.

———————————

NOTES:

< < What are Declarative and Interrogative Sentences? > >

Sentences are classified according to their purpose. A **declarative sentence** is a sentence that makes a statement.

Columbus discovered America in 1492.

An **interrogative sentence** is a sentence that asks a question.

Who discovered America?

When did Columbus discover America?

In English: To change a statement (S) into a question (Q), you sometimes need the helping verb (auxiliary) *do/does/did* before the subject. This auxiliary verb often serves to alert you that what follows is a question.

S: Paul and Mary go out together.
Q: *Do* Paul and Mary go out together?

S: Mark likes pretty girls.
Q: *Does* Mark like pretty girls?

S: Frank and June just got married.
Q: *Did* Frank and June just get married?

Another way to make a question is to switch the verb and the subject around, placing the verb before the subject.

S: *They are* home this evening.
Q: *Are they* home this evening?

Notice that in written English an interrogative sentence always has a question mark at the end.

In Spanish: A declarative sentence (S) can become an interrogative sentence (Q) by placing the subject after the verb; the word order of the question is **verb + subject**.

In written Spanish the question is signalled at both the beginning and end of the sentence. The punctuation mark at the beginning of the sentence is an upside-down question mark; a question mark like the one in English is located at the end of the sentence.

Statement	→	Question
Juan estudia.	→	¿Estudia Juan?
subject verb		verb subject
John studies.		*Does John study?*
Los chicos cantan.	→	¿Cantan los chicos?
subject verb		verb subject
The children sing.		*Are the children singing?*

NOTE: Be sure to ignore the auxiliary verbs *does/do/did* when using Spanish. Spanish has no such helping verbs.

When a statement consists of a subject and verb plus one or two words, those few words are usually placed between them. The word order of the question is **verb + remainder + subject**.

Statement	→	Question
Juan estudia español.	→	¿Estudia español Juan?
subject verb remainder		verb remainder subject
John studies Spanish.		*Does John study Spanish?*
La casa es grande.	→	¿Es grande la casa?
subject verb remainder		verb remainder subject
The house is big.		*Is the house big?*
Los chicos cantan bien.	→	¿Cantan bien los chicos?
subject verb remainder		verb remainder subject
The boys sing well.		*Do the boys sing well?*

In English and in Spanish you can also transform a statement into a question by adding a short phrase at the end of the statement. This short phrase is called a **tag** or **tag question**.

In English: The tag question repeats the idea of the statement in a negative way.

> John is a nice guy, *isn't he*?
> We study a lot, *don't we*?

The end part of the statement (*isn't he, don't we*) is the tag or tag question.

In Spanish: The words ¿no?, ¿verdad? or ¿no es verdad? can be added to a statement to form a tag question.

> Juan es un buen chico, ¿no?
> *John is a nice guy, isn't he?*

> Trabajas mucho, ¿verdad?
> *You work hard, don't you?*

> Hoy es miércoles, ¿no es verdad?
> *Today is Wednesday, isn't it?*

NOTES:

< < What are Affirmative and Negative Sentences? > >

Sentences are classified as to whether they agree or do not agree with the information they contain. An **affirmative sentence** agrees with the information it contains; it *affirms* the information.

> John works in a factory.
> Spain is a country in Europe.
> They like to travel.

A **negative sentence** does not agree with the information it contains; it *negates* the information.

> John does not work in a shoe store.
> Spain is not a country in Asia.
> They do not like to travel by bus.

In English: An affirmative sentence can become a negative sentence

- by adding the word *not* after the verb.

Affirmative	→	Negative
John is a student.	→	John is *not* a student.
They are here right now.	→	They are *not* here right now.

Frequently the word *not* is attached to the verb and the letter "o" is replaced by an apostrophe; this is called a **contraction**.

> John *isn't* a student.
> (is not)

> They *aren't* here right now.
> (are not)

- by adding the auxiliary verbs *do/does/did* + *not* + **the main verb in the infinitive** or dictionary form. (See **What is an Infinitive?**, p. 16.)

Affirmative	→	Negative
We study a lot.	→	We *do not study* a lot.
Julia writes well.	→	Julia *does not write* well.
The train arrived.	→	The train *did not arrive.*

In Spanish: The procedure for turning an affirmative sentence (**A**) into a negative sentence (**N**) is much more simple than in English. You merely place the word **no** in front of the conjugated verb.

Affirmative	→	Negative
Estudiamos mucho. *We study a lot.*	→	**No** estudiamos mucho. *We do **not** study a lot.*
Julia escribe bien. *Julia writes well.*	→	Julia **no** escribe bien. *Julia does **not** write well.*
El tren ha llegado. *The train arrived.*	→	El tren **no** ha llegado. *The train did **not** arrive.*

Remember that there is no equivalent for the auxiliary words *do/does/did* in Spanish; do not try to include them in a negative sentence.

NOTE: When answering a question negatively in English, both *no* and *not* will often appear in the answer.

> Do you live near the park?
> *No*, I do *not* live near the park.

Since both *no* and *not* have the Spanish equivalent **no**, when answering that same question negatively in Spanish, the word **no** will appear twice.

> ¿Vives cerca del parque?
> **No, no** vivo cerca del parque.

The first **no** answers the question; it has the English equivalent of *no*. The second **no** accompanies the verb; it has the English equivalent of *not*. Here is another example:

> *Do you have a blue car?*
> ¿Tienes un coche azul?

> *No, I do **not** have a blue car.*
> **No, no** tengo un coche azul.

< < What is Meant by Tense? > >

The **tense** of a verb means the time when the action of the verb takes place (at the **present** time, in the **past**, or in the **future**, for example).

> I *am eating.* Present
> I *ate.*   Past
> I *will eat.*   Future

As you can see in the above examples, just by putting the verb in a different tense and without giving any additional information (such as "I am eating *now*," "I ate *yesterday*," "I will eat *tomorrow*"), you can indicate when the action of the verb takes place.

< < What is the Present Tense? > >

The **present tense** indicates that the action is going on at the present time. It can be:

- at the time the speaker is speaking

  I *see* you.

- a habitual action

  He *smokes* when he *is* nervous.

- a general truth

  The sun *shines* every day.

In English: There are three forms of the verb which, although they have a slightly different meaning, all indicate the present tense.

Mary *studies* in the library.	Present
Mary *is studying* in the library.	Present progressive
Mary *does study* in the library.	Present emphatic

In Spanish: The **simple present tense** is used to express the meanings of the present, present progressive and present emphatic tenses in English. In Spanish the idea of present tense is indicated by the ending of the verb, without any auxiliary verb such as *is* and *does*. It is very important, therefore, not to translate these auxiliary verbs used in English. Simply put the main verb in the present tense.

Mary ***studies*** *in the library.*
      estudia

Mary ***is studying*** *in the library.*
      estudia

Mary ***does study*** *in the library.*
      estudia

There is a present progressive tense in Spanish but since it is not used in the same manner as the English present progressive, we have discussed it in a separate section. (See **What is a Progressive Tense?**, p. 50.)

< < What is the Past Tense? > >

The **past tense** is used to express an action that occurred in the past.

In English: There are several verb forms that indicate that the action took place in the past.

I worked	Simple past
I was working	Past progressive
I used to work	With helping verb *used to*
I did work	Past emphatic
I have worked	Present perfect
I had worked	Past perfect

In Spanish: There are many verb tenses which can be used to express an action which occurred in the past. Each tense has its own set of endings and its own rules which tell us when and how to use it. We will here be concerned with only two of the past tenses in Spanish: the **imperfect** (*el imperfecto*) and the **preterite** (*el pretérito*).

The **imperfect** is formed by adding certain endings to the stem. The conjugation is so very regular (there are only three irregular verbs in the imperfect) that there is no need to add to what is in your Spanish textbook on how to form the tense.

The **preterite** is also formed by adding certain endings to the stem. There are many irregular verbs in the preterite tense. It is very important to learn the preterite forms given in your textbook since the stems of the preterite are also used to form other verb tenses.

In choosing the correct tense in Spanish between the imperfect and the preterite, the English verb form will rarely tell you which tense the Spanish verb should be in. To select the right tense, you will have to rely on the rules given in your Spanish textbook.

In brief, the imperfect and the preterite take place at the same time in the past. However, when the duration of one action is compared to the <u>duration</u> of another action in the same sentence or story, the imperfect is used for the longer or more continuous of the two actions.

I *was reading* when he *came in.*
imperfect   preterite

Both actions are taking place at the same time, but the action of "reading" is continuous and the "coming in" just took an instant.

You might also note that there are two English verb forms that indicate when the imperfect should be used.

- If the English verb form includes, or could include, the helping verb *used to.*

   When I **was** a child I **sang.**

I sang has the same meaning as *I used to sing*; *I was* is a continuous action. Therefore, in Spanish, you use the imperfect for both verbs.

   Cuando **era** niño **cantaba.**
   imperfect   imperfect

- If the English verb form is in the **past progressive tense**, as *was laughing, were running.*

   *I **was working** all day long.*

   Trabajaba todo el día.
   imperfect

You should practice choosing the correct Spanish past tense with English texts, without translating them. Pick out the verbs in the past tense and indicate for each one if you would put it in the imperfect or in the preterite. Remember that selecting one of these two possible past tenses gives the verb a slightly different meaning. Sometimes both tenses are possible, but usually one of the two is more logical.

< < What is a Participle? > >

A **participle** has two functions: 1. It is a form of the verb that is used in combination with an auxiliary verb to indicate certain tenses. 2. It may be used as an adjective or modifier to describe something.

> I *was writing* a letter.
> auxiliary   participle

> The *broken* vase was on the floor.
>   participle describing *vase*

There are two types of participles: the **present participle** and the **past participle**. As you will learn in your study of Spanish, participles are not used in the same way in the two languages.

A. The **present participle**

In English: The present participle is easy to recognize because it is the *-ing* form of the verb: work*ing*, study*ing*, danc*ing*, play*ing*, etc.

The present participle is used:

- as the main verb in certain tenses

> She is *singing*.
> They were *dancing*.

- as an adjective

> This is an *amazing* discovery.
>   describes the noun *discovery*

> She read an *interesting* book.
>   describes the noun *book*

● as a modifier

> *Turning* the corner, Tony ran into a tree.
>
> The entire phrase *turning the corner* modifies or describes *Tony*.

> Look at the cat *climbing* the tree.
>
> *Climbing the tree* modifies the noun *cat*.

In Spanish: The present participle is formed by adding -ando to the stem of -ar verbs and -iendo to the stem of -er and -ir verbs. The -ndo of the Spanish participle corresponds to the -*ing* of the English present participle.

Infinitive	Stem	Present participle
cantar	cant-	cantando
comer	com-	comiendo
vivir	viv-	viviendo

There are some irregular forms which you will have to memorize individually. The present participle is used primarily in the formation of the progressive tenses. (See **What is a Progressive Tense?**, p. 50.)

B. The past participle

In English: It is formed in several ways. You can always find it by remembering the form of the verb you would use following *I have*: I have **spoken**, I have **written**, I have **walked**, etc.

The past participle is used:

● as an adjective

> Is the *written* word more important than the *spoken* word?
>
> *Written* describes the noun *word*.
> *Spoken* describes the noun *word*.

- as a verb form in combination with some form of the auxiliary verb *have*

  I *have written* all that I have to say.
  He *hasn't spoken* to me since our quarrel.

In Spanish: A verb can have a regular past participle, that is, a past participle formed according to the regular pattern: **-ar** verbs add **-ado** to the stem; **-er** and **-ir** verbs add **-ido** to the stem.

Infinitive	Stem	Past participle
hablar	habl-	hablado
comer	com-	comido
vivir	viv-	vivido

You will have to memorize irregular past participles individually. As you can see in the three examples below they are very different from the infinitive.

Infinitive	Stem	Past participle
romper	romp-	roto
escribir	escrib-	escrito
poner	pon-	puesto

As in English, the past participle can be used as an adjective or as a verb form.

- When the past participle is used as an adjective it must agree with the noun it modifies in gender and in number.

  the **closed** door

  Closed modifies the noun *door*.

  Since the Spanish word for *door* is feminine singular (**la puerta**) the word for *closed* in Spanish must also be feminine singular.

  la puerta **cerrada**

*the **broken** records*

Broken modifies the noun records.

Since the Spanish word for *records* is masculine plural (**los discos**) the word for *broken* must also be masculine plural.

los discos **rotos**

- The most important use of the past participle in Spanish is as a verb form in combination with the auxiliary verb **haber** to indicate a "perfect" tense. (See **What are the Perfect Tenses?**, p. 59.)

< < What is a Progressive Tense? > >

The **progressive tenses** are used to emphasize the moment that an action takes place or the continuation of the action.

John *is talking* on the phone.   (Now.)
We *were trying* to start the car.   (At that moment.)

In English: The progressive tenses are made up of the auxiliary verb *to be* + **the present participle of the main verb.**

We *are leaving* right now.
present tense   present participle
of *to be*

At that moment John *was washing* his car.
past tense   present participle
of *to be*

Notice that it is the tense of the auxiliary verb *to be* which indicates when the action of the main verb takes place.

In Spanish: The progressive tenses are made up of the auxiliary verb *estar* + **the present participle of the main verb**. A progressive form of the verb exists for all the tenses in Spanish. However, we shall here be concerned only with the present progressive. The **present progressive** is made up of the **present tense of** *estar* + **the present participle of the main verb**; it gives special emphasis to actions in progress.

- **Estamos saliendo** ahora mismo.
  present tense   present participle
  of **estar**

  We are leaving right now.

- ¿**Estás comiendo** ahora?
  present tense present participle
  of **estar**

  Are you eating now?

The progressive tenses are used far more frequently in English than in Spanish. Make sure that in Spanish you use them only when you want to emphasize that an action is happening at a particular moment or to stress the continuity of an action.

Compare the use of the present tense and present progressive tense in the sentences below.

- *John, what **are you studying** in school?*
  In Spanish: **estudias**

  present tense

  The present tense is used because you are asking what John is studying in general.

*John, what **are you studying** now?*

In Spanish: estás estudiando

present progressive

The present progressive is used because the word *now* indicates that you want to know what John is studying at this particular time as opposed to all other times.

- *Mary, **are you working** for the government?*

In Spanish: trabajas

present tense

The present tense is used because you are asking where Mary is working in general.

*Mary, **are you working** right now?*

In Spanish: estás trabajando

present progressive

The present progressive is used because the words *right now* indicate that you want to know if Mary is working at this particular time as opposed to all other times.

NOTE: Do not use the present progressive to state general truths or habitual action; use the present tense instead. (See **What is the Present Tense?**, p. 44.)

NOTES:

< < What is Meant by Mood? > >

The many forms a verb can take are divided into different **moods**. The word mood is a variation of the word *mode* meaning manner or way. The mood is the form of the verb which indicates the attitude (mode) of the speaker toward what he is saying. As a beginning student of Spanish, all you have to know are the names of the moods so that you will understand what your Spanish textbook is referring to. You will learn when to use the various moods as you learn verbs and their tenses.

In English: Verbs can be in one of three moods:

1. The **indicative mood** is used to express or indicate facts. This is the most common mood and most verb forms that you use in everyday conversation belong to the indicative mood.

    > Robert *studies* Spanish.
    > Mary *is* here.

    The present tense (see p. 44), the past tense (see p. 45), and the future tense (see p. 63) are all examples of tenses in the indicative mood.

2. The **imperative mood** is used to express a command. (See p. 55.)

    > Robert, *study* Spanish now!
    > Mary, *be* here on time!

3. The **subjunctive mood** is used to express a potential fact; it stresses the speaker's feelings about the fact and is "subjective" about those facts.

    > The professor insists that Robert *study* Spanish.
    > I wish that Mary *were* here.

In Spanish: The indicative and subjunctive moods exist. As in English, the indicative mood is the most common mood and most of the tenses you will learn belong to the indicative mood.

< < What is the Subjunctive? > >

The **subjunctive** mood exists in English, but it is used only in a few cases. It occurs in:

- contrary-to-fact statements

    If l *were* you, I would go on vacation.
    (But I'm not you.)
    She talked as though she *were* my boss.
    (But she isn't my boss.)

- statements expressing a wish that is not possible

    I wish it *were* not true.
    (But it is true.)
    I wish she *were* my teacher.
    (But she isn't my teacher.)

- the *that* clause following verbs of asking, demanding and recommending

    I recommend that he *take* the course.
    (Instead of "takes")
    I demanded that she *come* to see me.
    (Instead of "comes")

These are just a few examples to show you that English has the subjunctive form too.

In Spanish the subjunctive is used very frequently but unfortunately English usage will rarely help you decide where and how to use a subjunctive in your Spanish textbook. We encourage you to memorize the verb forms of the four subjunctive tenses (present, imperfect, present perfect, and pluperfect) and to learn the verbs, expressions and clauses which will require the use of a subjunctive verb form.

< < What is the Imperative? > >

The **imperative** is the command form of a verb. It is used to give someone an order.

In English: There are two types of commands:

1. The *you* **command** is used when giving an order to one person or many persons. The dictionary form of the verb is used for the *you* command.

> *Answer* the phone.
> *Clean* your room.
> *Talk* softly.

Notice that the pronoun "you" is not stated. The absence of the pronoun *you* in the sentence is a good indication that you are dealing with an imperative and not a present tense. Compare the following sentences:

Present tense (statement)	→	Imperative (command)
You answer the phone.	→	*Answer* the phone.
You clean your room.	→	*Clean* your room.
You talk softly.	→	*Talk* softly.

2. The *we* **command** is used when the speaker gives an order to himself as well as to others. In English this command begins with the phrase "let's" followed by the dictionary form of the verb.

> *Let's leave.*
> *Let's go* to the movies.

In Spanish: Spanish uses the same two basic types of commands: the *you* **command** and the *we* **command.**

The *you* **command.** The form you use depends on two factors:

1. Which form of "you" is appropriate in Spanish: **tú, vosotros/ vosotras, usted,** or **ustedes.** (See **What is Meant by Familiar and Formal You?**, p. 24.)

2. If you need a familiar *you* (**tú, vosotros/vosotras**) you will also have to determine if it is an affirmative command (an order to do something) or a negative command (an order not to do something).

   It is only after you have answered the above questions that you will be ready to select the correct command form in Spanish.

   Here are examples of each form:

- The *tú* **command** (familiar singular *you*) is used to give an order to a child, animal or a person you know well.

  The *affirmative* **tú** command has the same form as the 3rd person singular of the present tense.

¡Habla!	*Talk!*
¡Come!	*Eat!*
¡Escribe!	*Write!*

  There are several irregular forms which you will have to learn individually.

  The *negative* **tú** command has the same form as the 2nd person singular of the present subjunctive.

¡No hables!	*Don't talk!*
¡No comas!	*Don't eat!*
¡No escribas!	*Don't write!*

- The *vosotros* **command** (familiar plural *you*) is used to give an order to two or more persons you know well, children, or animals. These commands are used only in Spain.

The *affirmative* **vosotros** command is formed by dropping the -r from the infinitive ending and replacing it with a -d.

¡Hablad!	*Talk!*
¡Comed!	*Eat!*
¡Escribid!	*Write!*

The *negative* **vosotros** command has the same form as the 2nd person plural of the present subjunctive.

¡No habléis!	*Don't talk!*
¡No comáis!	*Don't eat!*
¡No escribáis!	*Don't write!*

- The *usted* **command** (formal singular *you*) is used to give an order to a person you do not know well.

The *affirmative* and *negative* **usted** commands have the same form as the 3rd person singular of the present subjunctive.

Affirmative		Negative	
¡Hable!	*Talk!*	¡No hable!	*Don't talk!*
¡Coma!	*Eat!*	¡No coma!	*Don't eat!*
¡Escriba!	*Write!*	¡No escriba!	*Don't write!*

- The *ustedes* **command** (formal plural *you* and in Latin America familiar plural *you*) which in Spain is used to give an order to more than one person that you do not know well and in Latin America to give an order to persons you do or do not know well.

The *affirmative* and *negative* **ustedes** command has the same form as the 3rd person plural of the present subjunctive.

Affirmative		Negative	
¡Hablen!	*Talk!*	¡No hablen!	*Don't talk!*
¡Coman!	*Eat!*	¡No coman!	*Don't eat!*
¡Escriban!	*Write!*	¡No escriban!	*Don't write!*

The use of the pronouns **usted** or **ustedes** following the command is optional. It is considered somewhat more polite to use the pronoun, but it is not rude to omit it.

- The *we* **command**.

  The *affirmative* and *negative* **nosotros** command has the same form as the first person plural of the present subjunctive.

  Affirmative

  ¡Hablemos!   *Let's talk!*
  ¡Comamos!   *Let's eat!*
  ¡Escribamos! *Let's write!*

  Negative

  ¡No hablemos!   *Let's not talk!*
  ¡No comamos!   *Let's not eat!*
  ¡No escribamos! *Let's not write!*

Notice that the English phrase *let's* does not translate in Spanish; the command ending is the equivalent of *let's*.

Here is a chart you can use as a reference.

Command Form	Affirmative	Negative
tú	Present indicative 3rd pers. sing.	Present subjunctive 2nd pers. sing.
vosotros	Infinitive -r → -d	Present subjunctive 2nd pers. pl.
usted	Present subjunctive 3rd pers. sing.	Present subjunctive 3rd pers. sing.
ustedes	Present subjunctive 3rd pers. pl.	Present subjunctive 3rd pers. pl.
nosotros	Present subjunctive 1st pers. pl.	Present subjunctive 1st pers. pl.

< < What are the Perfect Tenses? > >

The **perfect tenses** are compound verbs made up of the auxiliary verb *to have* + **the past participle** (See **What is a Participle?**, p. 47) **of the main verb.**

> I *have* not *seen* him.
> auxiliary verb   past participle of *to see*

> They *had* already *gone.*
> auxiliary verb   past participle of *to go*

As you can see, the auxiliary verb "to have" can be put in different tenses: for example, *I have* is the present tense; *they had* is the past tense.

In English: There are four perfect tenses formed with the auxiliary verb *to have* + **the past participle of the main verb.** The name of each perfect tense is based on the tense used for the auxiliary verb *to have.*

1. **present perfect**: *to have* in the *present* tense + the past participle of the main verb.

   > I *have eaten.*
   > auxiliary   past participle of *to eat*
   > verb

   > The boys *have washed* the car.
   > auxiliary   past participle of *to wash*
   > verb

2. **past perfect** (pluperfect): *to have* in the simple *past* tense + the past participle of the main verb.

   > I *had eaten* before 6:00.
   > auxiliary   past participle of *to eat*
   > verb

The boys *had* **washed** the car before the storm.

auxiliary   past particle of *to wash*
verb

3. **future perfect**: *to have* in the *future* tense + the past participle of the main verb. (See **What is the Future Tense?**, p. 63.)

I *will have* **eaten** by 6:00.

auxiliary   past participle of *to eat*
verb

The boys *will have* **washed** the car by Thursday.

auxiliary   past participle of *to wash*
verb

4. **conditional perfect**: *to have* in the *conditional* tense + the past participle of the main verb. (See **What is the Conditional Tense?**, p. 68.)

I *would have* **eaten** if I had had the time.

auxiliary verb   past participle of *to eat*

The boys *would have* **washed** the car if they had been here.

auxiliary verb   past participle of *to wash*

In Spanish: The perfect tenses are made up of a form of the auxiliary verb *haber* + **the past participle of the main verb.** In Spanish there are several perfect tenses: five perfect tenses in the indicative and two in the subjunctive. As in English, the name of the tense is based on the tense of the auxiliary verb **haber.**

We are listing the various perfect tenses here so that you can see the pattern which they follow. You will see that an entire section is devoted to the most common perfect tenses.

Perfect tenses in the indicative mood

1. **Present perfect** (*perfecto*): **haber** in the *present* tense + the past participle of the main verb.

> **He comido.**
> *I have eaten.*
>
> *Los chicos* **han lavado** *el coche.*
> *The boys* **have washed** *the car.*

Generally, the Spanish present perfect is used in the same way as the present perfect in English.

2. **Pluperfect or past perfect** (*pluscuamperfecto*): **haber** in the *imperfect* + the past participle of the main verb. The pluperfect tense is used to express an action completed in the past <u>before</u> some other past action or event.

> **Había comido** antes de las seis.
> *I had eaten before 6:00.*
>
> Los chicos **habían lavado** el coche antes de la tempestad.
> *The boys* **had washed** *the car before the storm.*

3. **Preterite perfect** (*pretérito perfecto*): **haber** in the *preterite* + the past participle of the main verb. This tense does not exist in English; in Spanish it is mainly a literary tense used to indicate a past action completed immediately before some other past action or event which was expressed by the preterite.

> Los chicos ya **hubieron lavado** el coche cuando llegó la tempestad.
>
> *The boys* **had** *already* **washed** *the car when the storm arrived.*

4. **Future perfect** (*futuro perfecto*): **haber** in the *future* + the past participle of the main verb. (See **What is the Future Tense?**, p. 63.)

> **Habré comido** para las seis.
> *I will have eaten by 6:00.*

Los chicos **habrán lavado** el coche para el jueves.
*The boys **will have washed** the car by Thursday.*

5. **Conditional perfect** (*condicional perfecto*): **haber** in the *conditional* tense + the past participle of the main verb. (See p. 70.)

Habría comido si hubiera tenido el tiempo.
*I **would have eaten** if I had had the time.*

Los chicos **habrían lavado** el coche si hubieran estado aquí.
*The boys **would have washed** the car if they had been here.*

Perfect tenses in the subjunctive mood (See **What is the Subjunctive?**, p. 54.)

1. **Present perfect subjunctive** (*perfecto del subjuntivo*): **haber** in the *present subjunctive* + the past participle of the main verb. This tense is really just a present perfect used when a subjunctive is required. Compare these two examples:

He knows that they *have arrived*.
In Spanish: present perfect
han llegado

He *hopes* that they *have arrived*.
In Spanish: present perfect subjunctive
hayan llegado

A subjunctive is used because *hopes* (the verb in the main clause) requires a subjunctive in the dependent clause.

2. **Pluperfect subjunctive** (*pluscuamperfecto del subjuntivo*): **haber** in the *imperfect subjunctive* + the past participle of the main verb. Compare these two examples.

He knew that they *had arrived*.
In Spanish: pluperfect
habían llegado

He *hoped* that they ***had arrived***.

In Spanish: pluperfect subjunctive

hubieran llegado

A subjunctive is needed because *hoped* (the verb in the main clause) requires a subjunctive in the dependent clause.

< < What is the Future Tense? > >

The **future tense** indicates that an action will take place sometime in the future.

In English: It is formed by means of the auxiliary *will* **or** *shall* **+ the main verb**.

Paul and Mary *will do* their homework tomorrow.
I *shall go* out tonight.

In Spanish: You do not need an auxiliary verb to show that the action will take place in the future. Future time is indicated by attaching different endings for each person to:

- the infinitive form of regular verbs

hablar-	-é	hablaré	*I will speak*
comer-	-á	comerá	*he will eat*

- special irregular future verb stems

(venir)	vendr-	vendré	*I will come*
(decir)	dir-	dirá	*he will talk*

Future of probability—In addition to expressing an action which will take place in the future, in Spanish the future tense can be used to express a probable fact, what the speaker feels is probably true. This is called the future of probability.

In English: The idea of probability is expressed with words such as *must, probably, wonder.*

> My keys *must* be around here.
> My keys are *probably* around here.
> I *wonder* if my keys are around here.

In Spanish: It is not necessary to use the words *must, probably,* or *wonder* to express probable facts; the main verb is simply put in the future tense.

- *I wonder who **is** at the door.*
    main verb
    present tense

    ¿ Quién **será** a la puerta?
    main verb
    future tense

- *It's probably my mother.*
    is main verb
    present tense

    Será mi madre.
    main verb
    future tense

- *I can't find my book. Carlos must **have** it.*
    main verb
    present tense

    No puedo encontrar mi libro. Carlos lo **tendrá**.
    main verb
    future tense

In English and in Spanish the fact that an action will occur some-time in the future can also be expressed without using the future tense.

In English: You can use the verb *to go* **in the present progressive+ the infinitive**. Thus,

> I *am going **to sing**.*
> present progressive   infinitive
>   of *to go*

means the same thing as

> I *will sing*.
>   future of *to sing*

In Spanish: You can use the verb *ir* (*to go*) **in the present tense + a + the infinitive**. Thus,

> *Voy* a **cantar**.
> present tense   infinitive
>   of **ir**

means the same thing as

> Cantaré.
> future tense of **cantar**

Notice that the "a" has no English equivalent; it must appear in the Spanish sentence however.

Here are other examples:

We will listen to the new records. future of *to listen*	*We are going to listen to the new records.* pres. progressive of *to go* + infinitive
Escucharemos los discos nuevos. future of **escuchar**	**Vamos a escuchar** los discos nuevos. pres. of **ir** + **a** + infinitive

In conversational Spanish **ir + a +** infinitive often replaces the future tense.

< < What is the Future Perfect? > >

The **future perfect** tense is used to express an action which will be completed in the future before some other specific action or event occurs in the future. It is used only when two actions will happen at different times in the future and you want to stress which one of the actions will come first.

In English: The future perfect is formed with the auxiliaries *will have* (or *shall have*) + **the past participle of the main verb.**

- I *will have eaten* before his arrival.

   future perfect   specific event in the future
   (2)   (1)

   Both action (2) and event (1) will occur at some future time, but action (2) will be completed before event (1) takes place. Therefore action (2) is in the future perfect tense.

- We *will have finished* by midnight.

   future perfect   specific event in the future
   (2)   (1)

   Action (2) will be completed before event (1) takes place. Therefore, action (2) is in the future perfect tense.

In Spanish: The future perfect is formed with a form of *haber* **in the future tense + the past participle of the main verb.**

It can be used to express an action which will be completed in the future before some other specific action or event occurs in the future.

- *I will have eaten before his arrival.*

   Habré comido antes de su llegada.

   future perfect   specific event in the future
   (2)   (1)

   Action (2) will be completed before event (1) takes place. Therefore action (2) is in the future perfect.

- *We **will have finished** by midnight.*

Habremos terminado para medianoche.
    future perfect   specific event in the future
         (2)   (1)

Action (2) will be completed before event (1) takes place. Therefore action (2) is in the future perfect.

NOTES:

< < What is the Conditional Tense? > >

The **conditional** tense is important in Spanish. Some modern English grammar books, however, do not include it. The use of the Spanish conditional and what we will call for our purposes the English "conditional" are sufficiently similar to justify a comparison.

NOTE: The use of the conditional in English and Spanish does not necessarily mean that the sentence implies a "condition."

In English: The **conditional** is a form of the verb composed of the auxiliary *would* + **the dictionary form of the main verb**. This is called the conditional tense.

> I said that I *would come* tomorrow.
> If she had the money, she *would call* him.
> I *would like* some ketchup, please.

NOTE: The auxiliary "would" in English has several meanings. It does not correspond to the conditional when it stands for *used to*, as in "She *would* talk while he painted." In this sentence, the verb means *used to* and requires the imperfect in Spanish.

The **conditional perfect** (See **What Are the Perfect Tenses?**, p. 59) is composed of the auxiliary *would have* + **the past participle of the main verb.**

> He *would have spoken*, if he had known the truth.
> If she had had the time, she *would have written* to him.
> I *would have eaten*, if I had been hungry.

The conditional is used in the following ways:

1. in the main clause of a **contrary-to-fact** (hypothetical or imaginary) statement.

> If I were rich, I *would buy* a Cadillac.

"I would buy a Cadillac" is called the **main clause**, or **result clause**. It is a **clause** because it is composed of a group of words containing a subject (*I*) and a verb (*would buy*) and is used as part of a sentence. It is the **main clause** because it expresses a complete thought and can stand by itself as a complete sentence.

"If I were rich" is called the **subordinate clause**, or **"if" clause**. Although it contains a subject (*I*) and a verb (*were*), it does not express a complete thought and can not stand alone.

2. in the subordinate clause to express a **future in the past**. (This means that the main clause must be in the past.)

> He said that he *would come.*
> (1)   (2)

Action (2) of the subordinate clause takes place after action (1). Therefore, action (2) is a future in the past and takes the conditional.

NOTE: If the main clause is in the present, then the future tense is used to express a future action.

> He *says* that he *will come.*
> present   future

3. for softened requests, a polite form with "like."

> I *would like* to eat.

This statement is more polite than "I *want* to eat."

In Spanish: You do not need an auxiliary verb to form the conditional; the **conditional** is indicated by attaching the endings of the imperfect tense for -er and -ir verbs (-ía, -ías, -ía, -íamos, -íais, -ían) to:

- the infinitive form of regular verbs

hablar-	-ía	hablaría	*I would talk*
vivir-	-íamos	viviríamos	*we would live*

- the special irregular future stems (see p. 63) such as

(poner)	pondr-	pondrían	*they would put*
(hacer)	har-	harías	*you would make*

The **conditional perfect** (*condicional perfecto*) is made up of a form of the auxiliary verb *haber* **in the conditional + the past participle of the main verb.**

habría hablado   *he would have spoken*
conditional   past participle
of **haber**   of **hablar**

The conditional is used

1. in the main or the result clause of a contrary-to-fact statement (the "if" clause contains the imperfect subjunctive)

   - *If she **had** the money, she **would buy** a car.*

     Si **tuviera** el dinero, **compraría** un coche.
     imperfect subjunctive   conditional

   - *If they **studied** more, they **would receive** better grades.*

     Si **estudiaran** más, **recibirían** notas mejores.
     imperfect subjunctive   conditional

2. in the subordinate clause to express a future in the past

   - *He **said** he **would come**.*
     past   conditional

     Dijo que **vendría**.
     preterite   conditional

- *I knew it* **would rain** *this evening.*
  /
  past   conditional

Sabía que **llovería** esta noche.
/
imperfect   conditional

The presence of "would" in the English sentences is a good indication of the need for a conditional in Spanish.

NOTE: Although in English a softened request is expressed with a conditional, in Spanish the softened request is indicated by the imperfect subjunctive.

    I **would like** *a glass of wine.*   (instead of: I want a glass of wine.)
     /
     conditional

    Quisiera un vaso de vino.
     /
     imperfect subjunctive

The conditional perfect is used in the result or main clause of a contrary-to-fact statement when the "if" clause is in the pluperfect subjunctive.

- *If she* **had had** *the money, she* **would have bought** *a car.*
       /
       past perfect   conditional perfect

    Si **hubiera tenido** el dinero, **habría comprado** un coche.
     /
     pluperfect subjunctive   conditional perfect

- *If they* **had studied** *more, they* **would have received** *better grades.*
       /
       past perfect   conditional perfect

    Si **hubieran estudiado** más, **habrían recibido** notas mejores.
     /
     pluperfect subjunctive   conditional perfect

Let us study some more contrary-to-fact statements in English to learn how to use them in Spanish.

How do you recognize a contrary-to-fact statement? It is always made up of two clauses:

1. the **"if" clause**, the clause that starts with *if* (**si** in Spanish)
2. the **result clause** or the **main clause**

The tense sequence is sometimes the same in Spanish and English.

"if" clause   result clause

1. present tense   +   future tense

     *If I **have** the money, I **will come**.*
      present   future

     Si tengo el dinero, **vendré**.

2. past tense (Eng.)   +   conditional
     imperfect subjunctive (Sp.)

     *If **I had** the time, **I would come**.*
       past   conditional

     Si tuviera el tiempo, **vendría**.
      imperfect sub.   conditional

3. past perfect (Eng.)   +   conditional perfect
     pluperfect subjunctive (Sp.)

     *If I **had had** the time, I **would have come**.*
      past perfect   conditional perfect

     Si hubiera tenido el tiempo, **habría venido**.
      pluperfect subjunctive   conditional perfect

In English and in Spanish the "if" clause can come either at the beginning of the sentence before the main clause, or at the end of the sentence. In the following examples observe how the tense used depends on the type of clause, <u>not</u> the clause order.

- *If she **were** rich, she**'d buy** a car.*
  past   conditional

  Si **fuera** rica, **compraría** un coche.
  imperfect subjunctive   conditional

  *She**'d buy** a car if she **were** rich.*
  conditional   past

  Compraría un coche si **fuera** rica.
  conditional   imperfect subjunctive

- *If she **had been** rich, she **would have bought** a car.*
  past perfect   conditional perfect

  Si **hubiera sido** rica **habría comprado** un coche.
  imperfect subjunctive   conditional perfect

  *She **would have bought** a car if she **had been** rich.*
  conditional perfect   past perfect

  Habría comprado un coche si **hubiera sido** rica.
  conditional perfect   pluperfect subjunctive

NOTES:

< < What is a Reflexive Verb? > >

A **reflexive verb** is a verb conjugated with a special pronoun called a **reflexive pronoun**; some textbook explanations say that the pronoun serves to "reflect" the action of the verb on the performer or subject.

> *She* cut *herself* with the knife.

> *He* saw *himself* in the mirror.

In English: The pronouns which end with *-self* or *-selves* are used to make verbs reflexive. Here are the reflexive pronouns.

myself	ourselves
yourself	yourselves
himself	
herself	themselves
itself	

Observe their usage in the following examples:

> *I* cut *myself.*

> *You* dried *yourself* with a towel.

> *Paul and Mary* blamed *themselves* for the accident.

In Spanish: The reflexive pronouns are:

me	*myself*
te	*yourself (fam. sing.)*
se	*himself, herself, yourself (form. sing.)*
nos	*ourselves*
os	*yourselves (fam. pl.)*
se	*themselves, yourselves (pl. form. and fam.)*

Certain verbs in Spanish are reflexive verbs. Reflexive verbs have an infinitive form which has the reflexive pronoun **se** attached to the end: **lavarse** (*to wash oneself*). In the dictionary the infinitive is listed as **lavarse** which is a separate verb from **lavar** (*to wash*). Since the reflexive pronoun reflects the action of the verb on the performer, the reflexive pronoun will change as the subject changes. When you learn to conjugate a reflexive verb, you will need to memorize the conjugation with the reflexive pronouns. Let's look at the conjugation of **lavarse** (*to wash oneself*) in the present tense; it is a regular -ar verb and it is a reflexive verb.

Subject pronoun	Reflexive pronoun	Verb form
yo	me	lavo
tú	te	lavas
él	se	lava
ella	se	lava
usted	se	lava
nosotros	nos	lavamos
vosotros	os	laváis
ellos	se	lavan
ellas	se	lavan
ustedes	se	lavan

Reflexive verbs can be conjugated in all tenses. The subject pronoun and reflexive pronoun remain the same regardless of the verb tense; only the verb form changes: **él se lavará** (*he will wash*), **él se lavó** (*he washed*).

Reflexive verbs are more common in Spanish than in English; that is, there are many verbs that take a reflexive pronoun in Spanish though not in English. For example, when you say in English, "Robert shaved" it is understood, but not stated, that "Robert shaved himself." In Spanish the "himself" has to be stated. The English verb *to get up* also has a reflexive meaning: "Mary got up" means that *she got herself up*. In Spanish you express *to get up* by using the verb **levantarse**, that is **levantar** (*to raise*) + the reflexive pronoun **se** (*oneself*). Similarly, some English expressions such as *to go to bed* are expressed in Spanish by a reflexive verb, in this case **acostarse**. You must memorize these reflexive verbs as they appear.

< < What is Meant by Active and Passive Voice? > >

Active voice and passive voice are terms used to describe the relationship between the verb and its subject.

In English:

The **active voice.** A verb is active when it expresses an action performed by the subject.

    The woman reads the novel.
       S   V   DO

    The boy closes the window.
       S   V   DO

    Lightning strikes the tree.
       S   V   DO

In all these examples the subject (S) performs the action of the verb (V) and the direct object (DO) is the receiver of the action.

The **passive voice.** A verb is passive when it describes the result of the action occurring in the active sentence.

    The novel is read by the woman.
       S   V   Agent

    The window is closed by the boy.
       S   V   Agent

    The tree is struck by lightning.
       S   V   Agent

In all these examples, the subject is not the performer of the action but is having the action performed upon it. Note also that the tense of the sentence is indicated by the tense of the auxiliary *to be*: "The novel *is* read by the woman" is in the present tense; whereas, "The novel *was* read by the woman" is in the past tense.

In Spanish: An active sentence can be changed to the true passive just as in English.

---

*The woman **reads** the novel.* → *The novel **is** read by the woman.*

La mujer **lee** la novela.   → La novela **es** leída por la mujer.
  S   V   DO   S   V   Agent
       present   present

You should note that

- all verbs in the passive are made up of a form of the auxiliary verb *ser* + **the past participle of the main verb.**

    La novela **es leída** por la mujer.

- the tense of the passive voice is indicated by the tense of the auxiliary verb **ser.**

    La ventana **es** cerrada por el chico.
    /
    present

    *The window **is** closed by the boy.*
    /
    present

    La ventana **fue** cerrada por el chico.
    /
    preterite

    *The window **was** closed by the boy.*
    /
    past

    La ventana **será** cerrada por el chico.
    /
    future

    *The window **will be** closed by the boy.*
    /
    future

- because the auxiliary verb in the passive is **ser**, the past participles become adjectives and must agree in gender and number with the noun they modify.

The novel was read by the woman.

La **novela** fue leída por la mujer.

   fem. sing.   fem. sing.

These buildings were constructed by my friend.

Estos **edificios** fueron construidos por mi amigo.

   masc. pl.   masc. pl.

- the agent is expressed by the word **por** meaning *by*.

Although Spanish has a passive voice it does not favor the use of it as English does. It is used infrequently, and generally in the preterite tense. Spanish speakers try to avoid the passive by using:

- the third person plural of the verb

    To avoid the passive construction, Spanish often makes "they" (the third person plural) the subject of an active sentence.

    The restaurant is opened at 5:00.

    > The restaurant is opened at 5:00. →
    > They open the restaurant at 5:00.

    Once you have transformed the English passive sentence to an English active form using "they" as subject, write it in Spanish.

Abren el restaurante a las cinco.

Each Christmas many presents are given.

> Each Christmas many presents are given. →
> Each Christmas they give many presents.

Cada Navidad dan muchos regalos.

- the **se** construction

In order to use the **se** construction as a replacement for the passive voice:

1. transform the English sentence using a reflexive form. (See **What is a Reflexive Verb?**, p. 74.)

The restaurant is opened at 5:00.	→	*The restaurant opens *itself* at 5:00.
Each Christmas many presents are given.	→	*Each Christmas many presents give *themselves*.
English is spoken here.	→	*English speaks *itself* here.

---

2. place the subject of the sentence after the verb in Spanish.

*The restaurant **opens itself** at 5:00.*
   subject   verb

Se abre el restaurante a las 5:00.

*Each Christmas many presents **give themselves**.*
             subject verb

Cada Navidad **se dan** muchos regalos.

*English **speaks itself** here.*
  subject   verb

Se habla inglés aquí.

Make sure that you find the subject of the sentence so that you make the verb agree with the subject; in the second sentence above the verb "**dan**" must agree with the subject "**regalos**". With passive sentences this is tricky because the subject is <u>after</u> the verb.

---

*An asterisk before a sentence means that the sentence is ungrammatical. The purpose of including such a sentence is to compare it to the Spanish one.

< < What is an Adjective? > >

An **adjective** is a word that describes a noun or a pronoun. Be sure that you do not confuse an adjective with a pronoun. A pronoun replaces a noun, while an adjective must always have a noun or a pronoun to describe.

In English: Adjectives describe nouns in many ways. They can tell:

- *what kind of noun it is* — **descriptive adjective**

    She lived in a *large* house.

    He has *brown* eyes.

- *whose noun it is* — **possessive adjective**

    His book is lost.

    Our parents are away.

- *which noun is it?* — **interrogative adjective**

    What book is lost?

    Which newspaper do you want?

- *which noun it is* — **demonstrative adjective**

    This teacher is excellent.

    That question is very appropriate.

In all these cases, it is said that the adjective modifies the noun.

There are also many examples of **nouns used as adjectives.**

Leather is expensive.   *Leather* goods are expensive.
   noun   adjective

The *desk* is black.   The *desk* lamp is black.
   noun   adjective

In Spanish: Adjectives are identified in the same way as in English. The most important difference is that when an adjective modifies a noun, that adjective must agree with the noun; that is, it must correspond in gender and number with the noun it describes. Also, the adjective usually is placed after the noun it modifies.

Looking only at descriptive adjectives for the time being, observe the agreement of the adjective in the following examples:

the red car	el coche rojo masc. sing. masc. sing.
the red cars	los coches rojos masc. pl. masc. pl.
the red table	la mesa roja fem. sing. fem. sing.
the red tables	las mesas rojas fem. pl. fem. pl.

Adjectives must agree in gender and number with the nouns they modify.

< < What is a Possessive Adjective? > >

A **possessive adjective** is a word which describes a noun by showing who possesses it.

In English: Here is a list of the possessive adjectives:

my	our
your	your
his, her, its	their

The possessive adjective refers only to the person who possesses.

>John's mother is young. *His* mother is young.
>Mary's father is rich. *Her* father is rich.
>The cat's ears are short. *Its* ears are short.

In Spanish: The front part of the possessive adjective refers to the possessor and the ending of the possessive adjective agrees with the item or person possessed. For example, in the phrase **nuestro hermano** (*our brother*) the front part of the possessive adjective **nuestr-** refers to a 1st person plural possessor *our*; the ending **-o** is masculine singular to agree with **hermano** which is masculine singular.

>nuestros **hermanos**
>
>1st pers. pl.   masc. pl. endings
>possessor: *our*

Like all adjectives in Spanish the possessive adjective must agree in number and gender with the noun it modifies.

Compare the agreement of these possessives in English and Spanish.

		Possessive form in Spanish
English:	We talk to *our* brother.	
Spanish:	We talk to *our brother*.	**nuestro hermano**
English:	We talk to *our* sister.	
Spanish:	We talk to *our sister*.	**nuestra hermana**
English:	We talk to *our* brothers.	
Spanish:	We talk to *our brothers*.	**nuestros hermanos**
English:	We talk to *our* sisters.	
Spanish:	We talk to *our sisters*.	**nuestras hermanas**

Let's look at the various forms of the Spanish possessive adjectives.

A. The possessive adjectives for *my, your* (fam. sing. form), *his, her, your* (form. sing. form), *their* and *your* (form. pl. form) have only two forms: singular and plural. These possessive adjectives have to change only in number in order to agree with the item possessed.

Here are the steps you should follow to choose these possessive adjectives:

1. Indicate the possessor.

	The possessive adjective will be
my	**mi**
your (fam. sing.)	**tu**
his	
her	
your (form. sing.)	**su**
their	
your (form. pl.)	

2. Make the possessive adjective agree with the item possessed.

   • If the item is singular, the form of the possessive adjective does not change.

I read my book.	Leo **mi** libro.
You read your book.	Lees **tu** libro.
He reads his book. *She reads her book.* *You read your book.*	Lee **su** libro.
They read their book. *You read your book.*	Leen **su** libro.

   • If the item is plural add -s to the possessive adjective.

I read my books.	Leo mis libros.
You read your books.	Lees tus libros.

*He reads **his** books.*
*She reads **her** books.* Lee sus libros.
*You read **your** books.*

*They read **their** books.*
*You read **your** books.* Leen sus libros.

B. The possessive adjectives for *our* and *your* (fam. pl. form) have four forms; they must change to agree in number and gender. Here are the steps you should follow to choose these possessive adjectives.

1. Indicate the possessor. This will be shown by the first letters of the possessive adjective.

   our the first letters will be **nuestr-**

   your the first letters will be **vuestr-**
   (fam. pl.)

2. Fill in the possessive adjective to agree with the item possessed.

   • If the item is masculine singular, add **-o.**

     Libro is masculine singular.

     *We read **our** book.* Leemos nuestro libro.

     *You read **your** book.* Leéis vuestro libro.

   • If the item is feminine singular, add **-a.**

     Revista is feminine singular.

     *We read **our** magazine.* Leemos nuestra revista.

     *You read **your** magazine.* Leéis vuestra revista.

- If the item is masculine plural, add **-os**.

  Libros is masculine plural.

  *We read **our** books.*   Leemos nuestros libros.

  *You read **your** books.*   Leéis vuestros libros.

- If the item is feminine plural, add **-as**.

  Revistas is feminine plural.

  *We read **our** magazines.*   Leemos nuestras revistas.

  *You read **your** magazines.*   Leéis vuestras revistas.

In Spanish as in English the subject and the possessive adjective do not necessarily have to match. It all depends on what you want to say.

- ¿Tiene **él su** libro?

  3rd person   3rd person
  singular   singular

  *Does **he** have **his** book?*

- ¿Tiene **él mi** libro?

  3rd person   1st person
  singular   singular

  *Does **he** have **my** book?*

- ¿Compraron **ellos su** coche?

  3rd person   3rd person
  plural   singular

  *Did **they** buy **her** car?*

NOTE: Before you write a sentence with *your* decide whether it is appropriate to use the **tú** (fam. sing.), **vosotros** (fam. pl.), **usted** (form. sing.) or **ustedes** (form. pl.) form in Spanish.

Then, make sure that your sentence is entirely in that form. For example, if the verb is in the **tú** form, the possessive adjective must also be in the **tú** form: "Lees tu libro." If the verb is in the **vosotros** form, the possessive adjective must also be in that form: "Leéis vuestro libro." If the verb is in the **usted** form, the possessive adjective must also be in the **usted** form: "Usted lee su libro." Be consistent since you cannot mix the various forms.

Spanish also has another set of possessive adjectives. The possessive adjectives of the second set follow the noun; they are called the **stressed possessive adjectives.** They add emphasis to the possessor and correspond to the English "of mine, of yours, " etc.: "that dress of mine" (instead of "my dress"), "those books of yours" (instead of "your books"). The use of these stressed adjectives is more common in Spanish than in English.

Like the unstressed possessives the front part of the stressed possessive adjective refers to the possessor and the ending agrees with the item or person possessed. For example, in the phrase **el libro tuyo** (*your book*) the front part of the possessive adjective **tuy-** refers to a 2nd person singular possessor *your*; the ending **-o** is masculine singular to agree with **libro** which is masculine singular.

Here is a list of the stressed possessive adjectives used with a masculine singular noun.

mío	*mine; of mine*
tuyo	*your; of yours*
suyo	*his, her, your; of his, of hers, of yours*
nuestro	*our; of ours*
vuestro	*your; of yours*
suyo	*their, your; of theirs, of yours*

In order to choose the proper form of the stressed possessive adjective follow the rules outlined for choosing the unstressed forms (pp. 82-85).

- *This car of mine doesn't work well.*

  masc. sing.   1st pers. sing.
  noun   possessor

  Este coche mío no funciona bien.

  masc. sing.   masc. sing.

- *These chairs of yours aren't very comfortable.*

  fem. pl.   2nd pers. sing.
  noun   possessor

  Estas sillas tuyas no son muy cómodas.

  fem. pl.   fem. pl.

NOTE: The stressed possessive adjectives have the same forms as the possessive pronouns. (See **What is a Possessive Pronoun?**, p. 129.)

< < What is an Interrogative Adjective? > >

An **interrogative adjective** is a word which asks a question about a noun.

In English: The words **which** and **what** are called interrogative adjectives when they come in front of a noun and are used to ask a question.

> *Which* book do you want?
> *What* dress do you want to wear?

In Spanish: There are two interrogative adjectives: **qué** which corresponds to the English **which** or **what** and the forms of **cuánto** meaning *how much* or *how many*.[1]

---

[1] In certain areas of the Spanish-speaking world **cuál** and **cuáles** can function as interrogative adjectives: ¿**Cuál** libro quieres? However, **qué** is the interrogative adjective *which/what* that is used in standard Spanish.

- *Which* or *what* + noun = **qué** + noun

Qué is invariable, that means that it never changes; it does not change form to agree in number and gender with the noun it modifies.

¿ **Qué** revista lees?   *What magazine are you reading?*
¿ **Qué** libros quieres?   *Which books do you want?*

- *How much* or *how many* + noun = **cuánto** + noun

Cuánto has four forms to agree in gender and number with the noun it modifies.

1. *How much money do you need?*

    Dinero is masculine singular, so that the word for *how much* is also masculine singular.

    ¿ **Cuánto** dinero necesitas?
    másc. sing.   másc. sing.

2. *How much soup do you want?*

    Sopa is feminine singular, so that the word for *how much* is also feminine singular.

    ¿ **Cuánta** sopa quieres?
    fem. sing.   fem. sing.

3. *How many records do you have?*

    Discos is masculine plural, so that the word for *how many* is also masculine plural.

    ¿ **Cuántos** discos tienes?
    masc. pl.   masc. pl.

4. *How many suitcases are you bringing?*

    Maletas is feminine plural, so that the word for *how many* is also feminine plural.

    ¿ **Cuántas** maletas traes?
    fem. pl.   fem. pl.

NOTE: Make sure you do not confuse interrogative adjectives and interrogative pronouns (see p. 120). The word *what* in "*What* is the Nobel Prize?" is an interrogative pronoun. As an interrogative pronoun **qué** is not followed by a noun: " ¿**Qué** es el Premio Nobel?" The words *how many* in "*How many* do you need?" are also interrogative pronouns; they are not followed by a noun: "¿**Cuántos** necesitas?" (See **What are Interrogative Pronouns?**, p. 120.)

< < What is a Demonstrative Adjective? > >

A **demonstrative adjective** is a word used to point out a noun.

In English: The demonstrative adjectives are ***this/that*** and ***these/those***. They are a rare example of adjectives agreeing with the noun they modify: ***this*** changes to ***these*** before a plural noun and ***that*** changes to ***those***.

this cat	*these* cats
that man	*those* men

In Spanish: There are three sets of demonstrative adjectives; each set has four forms because they must agree in gender and number with the nouns they modify: a masculine and feminine form in the singular to agree with singular nouns and a masculine and feminine form in the plural to agree with plural nouns.

1. Forms to point out a noun <u>near the speaker</u>.

this *room*	**este** cuarto	(masc. sing.)
this *house*	**esta** casa	(fem. sing.)
these *rooms*	**estos** cuartos	(masc. pl.)
these *houses*	**estas** casas	(fem. pl.)

If you want to say "*this* book" in Spanish, begin by analyzing the Spanish equivalent for the word "book."

*Do you see **this** book?*

> **Libro** is masculine singular, so that the word for *this* is also masculine singular.

¿Ves **este** libro?

masc. sing.   masc. sing.

Similarly for "*these* tables" begin by analyzing the Spanish equivalent for the word "tables."

> *Do you see **these** tables?*

> **Mesas** is feminine plural, so that the word for *these* is also feminine plural.

¿Ves **estas** mesas?

fem. pl.   fem. pl.

2. Forms to point out a noun which is <u>near the person spoken to.</u>

***that** room*	**ese** cuarto	(masc. sing.)
***that** house*	**esa** casa	(fem. sing.)
***those** rooms*	**esos** cuartos	(masc. pl.)
***those** houses*	**esas** casas	(fem. pl.)

If you want to say "*that* table" in Spanish, begin by analyzing the Spanish equivalent for "table."

> *Do you see **that** table?*

> **Mesa** is feminine singular, so that the word for *that* is also feminine singular.

¿Ves **esa** mesa?

fem. sing.   fem. sing.

Similarly, if you want to say "*those* books" begin by analyzing the Spanish equivalent for "books."

*Do you see **those** books?*

> **Libros** is masculine plural, so that the word for *those* is also masculine plural.

¿Ves **esos** libros?

masc. pl.   masc. pl.

3. Forms to point out a noun which is <u>away from the speaker and the person spoken to</u>.

***that** room*	**aquel** cuarto	(masc. sing.)
***that** house*	**aquella** casa	(fem. sing.)
***those** rooms*	**aquellos** cuartos	(masc. pl.)
***those** houses*	**aquellas** casas	(fem. pl.)

If you want to say "*that* book" in Spanish, begin by analyzing the Spanish equivalent for "book."

> *Do you see **that** book?*

> **Libro** is masculine singular, so that the word for *that* is also masculine singular.

¿Ves **aquel** libro?

masc. sing.   masc. sing.

Similarly, if you want to say "*those* tables" in Spanish, begin by analyzing the Spanish equivalent for "tables."

> *Do you see **those** tables?*

> **Mesas** is feminine plural, so that the word for *those* is also feminine plural.

¿Ves **aquellas** mesas?

fem. pl.   fem. pl.

NOTE: The three sets of demonstrative adjectives may also function as demonstrative pronouns. As demonstrative pronouns they carry a written accent and are not followed by a noun. (See **What are Demonstrative Pronouns?**, p. 125.)

< < What is Meant by Comparison of Adjectives? > >

When adjectives are used to compare the qualities of the nouns they modify, they change forms. This change is called **comparison.**

comparison of adjectives

John is tall but Anthony is taller.

adjective modifying   adjective modifying
the noun *John*   the noun *Anthony*

There are three types of comparison: **positive, comparative** and **superlative.**

In English: Let us go over what is meant by the different types of comparison and how each type is formed.

1. The positive form refers to the quality of one person or thing. It is simply the adjective form.

    Mary is *pretty*.
    My house is *big.*
    His car is *expensive*.
    This book is *interesting.*

2. The comparative form compares the quality of one person or thing with another person or thing. It is formed:

    - by adding *-er* to short adjectives.

      Mary is *prettier* than Ann.
      My house is *bigger* than his.

    - by placing ***more*** (or ***less***) in front of longer adjectives and ***than*** after.

      His car is *more expensive than* mine.
      This book is *less interesting than* that one.

3. The superlative form is used to stress the highest degree of a quality. It is formed:

- by adding **-est** to short adjectives.

  Mary is the *prettiest* in the family.
  My house is the *biggest* on the street.

- by placing **the most** (or **the least**) in front of longer adjectives.

  His car is *the most expensive* in the race.
  This book is *the least interesting* of all.

A few adjectives do not follow this regular pattern of comparison. You must use an entirely different word for the comparative and the superlative.

This apple is bad.	(positive)
This apple is worse.	(comparative)
not *badder	
This apple is the worst.	(superlative)
not *baddest	

In Spanish: There are the same three types of comparisons as in English.

1. The positive is simply the adjective form.

   María es **bonita**.
   *Mary is **pretty***.

   Mi casa es **grande**.
   *My house is **big***.

   Su coche es **caro**.
   *His car is **expensive***.

   Este libro es **interesante**.
   *This book is **interesting***.

---

*An asterisk means that what follows is ungrammatical.

2. The comparative is formed by adding **más** or **menos** in front of the adjective and **que** after:

$$\genfrac{}{}{0pt}{}{\textit{más}}{\textit{menos}} + \textbf{adjective} + \textit{que}$$

   María es **más bonita que** Ana.
   *Mary is **prettier than** Ann.*

   Mi casa es **más grande que** la suya.
   *My house is **bigger than** his.*

   Su coche es **más caro que** el mío.
   *His car is **more expensive than** mine.*

   Este libro es **menos interesante que** ése.
   *This book is **less interesting than** that one.*

3. The superlative is formed by adding the definite article which corresponds in gender and number to the noun described and **más** or **menos** in front of the adjective and **de** after the adjective:

$$\textbf{definite article} + \genfrac{}{}{0pt}{}{\textit{más}}{\textit{menos}} + \textbf{adjective} + \textit{de}$$

   María es **la más bonita de** la familia.
   *Mary is **the prettiest** in the family.*

   Mi casa es **la más grande de** la calle.
   *My house is **the biggest** on the street.*

   Su coche es **el más caro de** la carrera.
   *His car is **the most expensive** in the race.*

   Este libro es **el menos interesante de** todos.
   *This book is **the least interesting** of all.*

As in English there are a few forms that you will have to memorize individually. For example:

> Esta manzana es **mala**. (positive)
> *This apple is **bad**.*
>
> Esa manzana es **peor**. (comparative)
> *That apple is **worse**.*
>
> Aquella manzana es **la peor**. (superlative)
> *That apple is **the worst**.*

The preceding comparisons were comparisons of inequality: the things compared were different or unequal. Let's now look at **comparisons of equality**: the things compared are the same or equal.

In English: Comparisons of equality are expressed with the words *as* + **adjective** + *as*. The comparison can be between two people or several.

> John is *as tall as* Joe.
>   adjective
>
> Mary is *as intelligent as* her friends.
>   adjective

In Spanish: Comparisons of equality are expressed with the words *tan* + **adjective** + *como*.

> Juan es **tan alto como** José.
> *John is **as tall as** Joe.*

NOTE: Adverbs (see **What is an Adverb?**, p. 99) are compared in the same manner as adjectives in both English and Spanish. Adverbs are invariable; that is, they do not change form to agree with the verb they modify.

< < What is a Preposition? > >

A **preposition** is a word which shows the relationship between a noun and another word in the sentence. Prepositions may indicate position, direction or time.

In English: Here are examples of some prepositions:

- to show position

    > Bob was *in* the car.
    > The books are *on* the table.

- to show direction

    > Mary went *to* school.
    > The students came directly *from* class.

- to show time

    > French people go on vacation *in* August.
    > Their son will be home *at* Christmas.

In Spanish: You will have to memorize prepositions as vocabulary items. There are three important things to remember:

1. Prepositions are **invariable**. This means that their spelling never changes. (They never become plural, nor do they have a gender.)

2. Prepositions are tricky little words. Every language uses prepositions differently. Do not assume that the same preposition is used in Spanish as in English or that one is even used at all.

English	Spanish

preposition → no preposition

| to look *for* | buscar |
| to look *at* | mirar |

no preposition → preposition

| to leave | salir **de** |
| to enter | entrar **en** |

change of preposition

| to laugh *at* | reirse **de** (*of*) |
| to consist *of* | consistir **en** (*in*) |

3. Although the position of a preposition in an English sentence may vary, it cannot in Spanish. Look at the position of the preposition in the following English phrases.

Spoken English	→ Formal English
The man I speak *to*	→ The man *to* whom I speak
Who are you playing *with*?	→ *With* whom are you playing?
The teacher I'm talking *about*	→ The teacher *about* whom I'm talking

Spoken English tends to place the preposition at the end of the sentence. Formal English places the preposition within the sentence or at the beginning of a question.

The position of a preposition in a Spanish sentence is the same as in formal English; that is, it is <u>never</u> at the end of a sentence. Whenever you have a preposition at the end of an English sentence, be sure to change the structure.

There are some English expressions where the natural position of the preposition is at the end of the sentence; it is not a question of spoken or written language.

We have much to be thankful *for*.

Changing the prior structure by placing the preposition within the sentence may sound awkward.

We have much *for* which to be thankful.

However, in Spanish, it is still necessary to reword the sentence to include the preposition within the sentence. This rearranging of the preposition will be very helpful to you. It will help you to determine the function of words and the word order in the Spanish sentence.

NOTE: A special word needs to be said about the preposition **de** (*of, from*) in Spanish, because it is used in structures that do not exist in English.

1. When a noun is used as an adjective to describe another noun (see p. 80) **de** is used as follows:

   - **the noun described + *de* + the describing noun used without an article**

A	B
los libros **de** química	*the chemistry books*
la clase **de** español	*the Spanish class*
el aceite **de** oliva	*the olive oil*

     The noun in Column B gives information about the noun in Column A.

2. When a noun possesses another noun (see pp. 12-13) **de** is used as follows:

   - **the noun possessed + *de* + definite article + the noun that possesses**

A	B
el coche **del** señor	*the man's car*

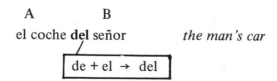

de + el → del

el coche **de los** señores	*the men's car*
el coche **de la** señora	*the lady's car*
el coche **de las** señoras	*the ladies' car*

The noun in Column A belongs
to the noun in Column B.

When the noun that possesses is a name no article is used:

el coche **de** Juan	*John's car*
la casa **de** María Gómez	*María Gómez' house*

< < What is an Adverb? > >

An **adverb** is a word that modifies (describes) a verb, an adjective
or another adverb. Adverbs indicate quantity, time, place, intensity and manner.

Mary drives *well*.
    verb

The house is *very* big.
       adjective

The girl ran *too* quickly.
       adverb

In English: Here are some examples of adverbs:

- of quantity or degree

    Mary sleeps *little*.
    Bob does *well enough* in class.

These adverbs answer the question *how much*.

- of time

> He will come **soon**.
> The children are **late**.

These adverbs answer the question *when*.

- of place

> The teacher looked **around**.
> The old were left **behind**.

These adverbs answer the question *where*.

- of intensity

> Bob **really** wants to learn Spanish.
> Mary can **actually** read Latin.

These adverbs are used for *emphasis*.

- of manner

> Bob sings **beautifully**.
> They parked the car **carefully**.

These adverbs answer the question *how*. They are the most common adverbs and can usually be recognized by their **-ly** ending.

In Spanish: You will have to memorize most adverbs as vocabulary items. Most adverbs of manner can be recognized by the ending **-mente** which corresponds to the English ending **-ly**.

natural**mente**	*naturally*
general**mente**	*generally*
rápida**mente**	*rapidly*

The most important thing for you to remember is that adverbs are **invariable**: this means that the spelling never changes. (Adverbs never become plural, nor do they have gender.) For this reason, it is necessary that you distinguish adverbs from adjectives which do change. When you write a sentence in Spanish, always make sure that the adjectives agree with the noun or pronoun they modify and that adverbs remain unchanged.

- *The **tall** girl talked **rapidly**.*

    Tall modifies the noun *girl*; it is an adjective.

    Rapidly modifies the verb *talked*; it describes how she talked; it is an adverb.

    La **chica alta** habló **rápidamente**.
    fem. sing.

- *The **tall** boy talked **rapidly**.*

    Tall modifies the noun *boy*; it is an adjective.

    Rapidly modifies the verb *talked*; it describes how he talked; it is an adverb.

    El **chico alto** habló **rápidamente**.
    masc. sing.

NOTE: Remember that in English *good* is an adjective; *well* is an adverb.

    The boy is *good*.   (He behaves properly.)

    Good modifies *boy*; it is therefore an adjective.

    The boy is *well*.   (He isn't sick.)

    Well modifies *is*; it is therefore an adverb.

Likewise, in Spanish **bueno** is an adjective meaning *good*; **bien** is the adverb meaning *well*.

    *The **good** girl sang **well**.*
    adjective   adverb

    La chica **buena** cantó **bien**.
    fem. sing.   adverb

< < What is a Conjunction? > >

A **conjunction** is a word which joins words or groups of words.

Paul plays basketball *and* tennis.
We'll go to the movies *or* the theater.
I liked neither the book *nor* the play.
The children are happy *whenever* he comes.

Conjunctions are to be memorized as vocabulary items. Remember that like adverbs and prepositions, conjunctions are **invariable**; they never change. (They never become plural, nor do they have a gender.)

< < What are Objects? > >

Every sentence consists, at the very least, of a subject and a verb. This is called the **sentence base**.

Children play.
Work stopped.

The subject of the sentence is a noun or pronoun. Most sentences contain other nouns or pronouns, however. Many of the nouns or pronouns in a sentence function as **objects**. These objects are divided into three categories depending upon their position in the sentence and how they are used. The three types of objects are:

1. direct object
2. indirect object
3. object of a preposition

1. Direct object and 2. Indirect object

In English:

1. **Direct object**: It receives the action of the verb or shows the result of that action directly, without prepositions separating the verb from the receiver. It answers the **one-word question** *what?* or *whom?* asked after the verb.

    ● Paul writes *a letter*.

    > Paul writes what? A letter.
    > *A letter* is the direct object.

    ● They see *Paul and Mary*.

    > They see *whom*? Paul and Mary.
    > *Paul and Mary* are the two direct objects.

Never assume that a word is the direct object. Always ask the one-word question and if you don't get an answer, you don't have a direct object in the sentence.

John writes well.

> John writes what? No answer.
> John writes whom? No answer.

There is no direct object in this sentence. *Well* is an adverb.

2. **Indirect object**: It explains "to whom" or "to what" or "for whom" or "for what" the action of the verb is done. It answers the **two-word question** *to whom?/to what?* or *for whom?/for what?* asked after the verb.

    ● John writes *his brother*.

    > John writes to whom? To his brother.
    > *His brother* is the indirect object.

    ● Susan did *me* a favor.

    > Susan did a favor for whom? For me.
    > *Me* is the indirect object.

Sometimes the word *to* is included in the English sentence.

> John speaks to ***Paul and Mary***.
>
> > John speaks to whom? To Paul and Mary.
> > *Paul and Mary* are the two indirect objects.[1]

In Spanish:

1. **Direct object**: As in English, the Spanish direct object receives the action of the verb or shows the result of that action.

   > Pablo escribe **una carta**.
   > *Paul writes **a letter**.*

   In Spanish when the direct object of the verb is a person it is preceded by the word **a**. This is called the **personal a.**

   - Juan ve **a las muchachas**.
     *John sees **the girls**.*

   - Juan ve **al** hombre.

     > | a + el → al |
     > |---|

     *John sees **the man**.*

   BUT: Juan ve **la casa**.
   *John sees **the house**.*

2. **Indirect object**: As in English the Spanish indirect object explains "to whom" or "to what" or "for whom" or "for what" the action of the verb is done. The English word *to* or *for* is expressed by **a** in Spanish.

   > Juan escribe **a su hermano**.
   > *Juan writes (**to**) **his brother**.*

---

[1] Although "to Paul and Mary" functions grammatically as a prepositional phrase, we will retain the term indirect object for ease of identification since that is how it functions in Spanish. All similar patterns will be called indirect objects.

Susana hizo un favor **a Ana.**
*Susan did **Ann** a favor.*

Juan habla **a Pablo y a María.**
*John speaks **to Paul and Mary**.*

It is essential that you learn to distinguish direct and in-direct objects especially when dealing with pronouns. For example, the word *him* in Spanish will have two forms depending on whether "him" is a direct object (**lo**) or indirect object (**le**). Since the word "**a**" is used not only before an indirect object but also before a direct object referring to a person, it is often difficult to distinguish the two types of objects in a Spanish sentence.

How can you distinguish a direct from an indirect object?

Use the English translation as a guide. Ask yourself if the English sentence contains or could contain the word *to* (or *for*) before the object. If yes, it is an indirect object; if no, it is a direct object.

- Juan habla a María.
  Can the word *to* be placed before the object? Yes.
  John speaks *to* Mary.

  Mary is the indirect object.

- Juan escribe a sus amigos.
  Can the word *to* be placed before the object? Yes.
  John writes *to* his friends.

  His friends is the indirect object.

- Juan ve a María.
  Can the word *to* be placed before the object? No.
  *John sees *to* Mary cannot exist in English.
  John sees Mary.

  Mary is the direct object.

A sentence may contain both a direct object and an indirect object.

---

*An asterisk before a sentence means that the sentence is ungrammatical. The purpose of including such a sentence is to compare it to a correct sentence.

In English: When both objects are present the indirect object usually precedes the direct object; the following word order is found in an affirmative sentence:

Subject + Verb + Indirect Object + Direct Object

- Paul wrote his brother a letter.

    S   V   IO   DO

        Paul wrote *what*? A letter.
        A letter is the direct object.

        Paul wrote *to whom*? To his brother.
        His brother is the indirect object.

- Susan did Ann a favor.

    S   V   IO   DO

        Susan did *what*? A favor.
        A favor is the direct object.

        Susan did a favor *for whom*? For Ann.
        Ann is the indirect object.

These two sentences could also be written using another word order:

Subject + Verb + Direct Object + *to* (or *for*) + Indirect Object

        Paul wrote a letter to his brother.
        S   V   DO to   IO

        Susan did a favor for Ann.
        S   V   DO for IO

In Spanish: There is only one pattern for sentences containing a direct and an indirect object as long as both objects are nouns. The pattern is the same as the optional English pattern with the word *to* + indirect object at the end of the sentence:

Subject + Verb + Direct Object + *a* + Indirect Object

Pablo	escribe	una carta	a	su hermano.
Paul	*writes*	*a letter*	*to*	*his brother.*

Make sure that you place the direct object before the indirect object before expressing the sentence in Spanish.

Martha gave the girl a present.

    IO   DO

> Martha gave the girl a present. → Martha gave a present to the girl.

Marta dio un regalo a la muchacha.

        DO   IO

3. Object of a Preposition

In English: The noun or pronoun which follows the preposition (See **What is a Preposition?**, p. 96) is called the **object of the preposition**. The object of the preposition answers a **two-word question** made up of the **preposition** + *what or whom*.

The book is ***in the desk.***

The book is *in what*? In the desk.
The desk is the object of the preposition *in*.

John is leaving ***with Mary***.

John is leaving *with whom*? With Mary.
Mary is the object of the preposition *with*.

In Spanish: Objects of a preposition are as easy to identify as in English. The above two sentences in Spanish read as follows:

El libro está **en el escritorio**.
*The book is **in the desk**.*

Juan sale **con María**.
*John is leaving **with Mary**.*

Make sure that you recognize prepositions in Spanish.

As a student of Spanish you must watch out for the following pitfall: some English verbs that take a preposition and object of a preposition require a direct object in Spanish. This is because a verb may require a preposition in one language but not in the other.

- *to wait **for*** — esperar

> *John **waits for** the bus.*
>> John waits *for what*? The bus.
>> *The bus* is the object of the preposition *for*.

> Juan **espera** el autobús.
>> ¿Qué espera Juan? El autobús.
>> **El autobús** is the direct object; the word *for* is contained in the verb **espera**.

- *to listen **to*** — escuchar

> *John **listens to** the music.*
>> John listens *to what*? To the music.
>> *The music* is the object of the preposition *to*.

> Juan **escucha** la música.
>> ¿Qué escucha Juan? La música.
>> **La música** is the direct object; the word *to* is contained in the verb **escucha**.

Here are some verbs to watch out for:

*to look **for***	buscar
*to look **at***	mirar
*to ask **for***	pedir
*to listen **to***	escuchar
*to wait **for***	esperar
*to wait **on***	servir

< < What is an Object Pronoun? > >

Pronouns in English and in Spanish change according to their function in the sentence. The pronouns used as subject of a sentence are studied on p. 23. Let's look at pronouns used as objects.

In English: The pronouns that occur as objects in a sentence are called **object pronouns**. They are different from the pronouns used as subjects. Object pronouns are used when a pronoun is a direct object, indirect object or object of a preposition. (See **What are Objects?**, p. 102.)

> *He* works for the newspaper.
> subject - subject pronoun

> Mother saw *him* last night.
> direct object - object pronoun

> I lent *him* my car.
> indirect object - object pronoun

> They went to the movies with *him*.
> object of a preposition - object pronoun

Compare the English pronouns:

Subject	Object
I	me
you	you
he	him
she	her
it	it
we	us
you	you
they	them

In Spanish: Let's refresh your memory with the pronouns used as the subject of the sentence. (See p. 23.)

yo	*1st pers. sing.*
tú	*2nd pers. sing.*
él ⎫	
ella ⎬	*3rd pers. sing.*
usted ⎭	
nosotros/-as	*1st pers. pl.*
vosotros/-as	*2nd pers. pl.*
ellos ⎫	
ellas ⎬	*3rd pers. pl.*
ustedes ⎭	

Remember that the Spanish equivalent of *it* is either **él** or **ella** depending upon whether *it* replaces a masculine or feminine noun.

Direct and Indirect Object Pronouns

The same pronouns are used as both direct object pronouns and indirect object pronouns except in the 3rd person singular and plural. Let's first look at the 1st and 2nd persons.

Subject		Object
yo	*1st pers. sing.*	me
tú	*2nd pers. sing.*	te
nosotros/-as	*1st pers. pl.*	nos
vosotros/-as	*2nd pers. pl.*	os

The direct (**DO**) or indirect object (**IO**) pronoun is placed directly in front of a conjugated verb in Spanish.

- *John sees **us**.*
    John sees *what*? Us.
    Us is the direct object.
  Juan **nos** ve.
        DO

- *John sees **you**.*
  > John sees *whom*? You.
  > *You* is the direct object.

  Juan **te** ve.
  > DO

- *John writes **to me**.*
  > John writes *to whom*? To me.
  > *Me* is the indirect object.

  Juan **me** escribe.
  > IO

- *John writes **to you**.*
  > John writes *to whom*? To you.
  > *You* is the indirect object.

  Juan **os** escribe.
  > IO

NOTE: The *to* preceding the English indirect object is not expressed in Spanish when a pronoun is used; the Spanish indirect object pronoun means *to me, to you,* etc. so there is no need for the equivalent of *to*.

The pronouns of the 3rd person, the ones that are the equivalent of *him, her, it, them,* change according to whether they are used as direct or indirect objects and according to the gender and number of the noun they replace.

		Subject	Direct Object	Indirect Object
Singular	*Masculine*	él	lo	le
	Feminine	ella	la	le
		usted		
Plural	*Masculine*	ellos	los	les
	Feminine	ellas	las	les
		ustedes		

It can be (1) a subject, (2) direct or indirect object or (3) object of a preposition. You must, therefore, establish the function of *it* in the sentence and determine the gender of the noun it replaces in order to choose the correct Spanish equivalent.

- *Where is the book? It is on the table.*

    Function: subject of *is*
    Noun it replaces: the book (**el libro**)
    Gender in Spanish: masculine

    Therefore, *it* = **él.**

  ¿Dónde está el libro? El está sobre la mesa.

- *Where is the table? It is in the living room.*

    Function: subject of *is*
    Noun it replaces: the table (**la mesa**)
    Gender in Spanish: feminine

    Therefore, *it* = **ella.**

  ¿Dónde está la mesa? Ella está en la sala.

- *Do you see the book? Yes, I see it.*

    Function: direct object
    Noun it replaces: the book (**el libro**)
    Gender in Spanish: masculine

    Therefore, *it* = **lo.**

  ¿Ves el libro? Sí, **lo** veo.

- *Do you see the table? Yes, I see it.*

    Function: direct object
    Noun it replaces: the table (**la mesa**)
    Gender in Spanish: feminine

    Therefore, *it* = **la.**

  ¿Ves la mesa? Sí, **la** veo.

Him or *her* can be (1) a direct object or (2) an indirect object. You must determine how the word *him* or *her* functions in order to choose the correct pronoun. Let's look at some examples.

- *Do you see Robert? Yes, I see **him**.*
  *Do you see Mary? Yes, I see **her**.*

    Function: direct object (You see *whom*? Robert, Mary.)

    Therefore, ***him*** = **lo**.
           her = **la**.

  ¿Ves a Roberto? Sí, **lo** veo.
  ¿Ves a María? Sí, **la** veo.

- *Are you giving Paul the book? Yes, I'm giving **him** the book.*
  *Are you giving Mary the book? Yes, I'm giving **her** the book.*

    Function: indirect object (I give the book *to whom*?
                   To him, to her.)

    Therefore, ***him*** = **le**.
           her = **le**.

  ¿Das el libro a Pablo? Sí, **le** doy el libro.
  ¿Das el libro a María? Sí, **le** doy el libro.

In order to distinguish **le** meaning ***to him*** from **le** meaning ***to her***, the phrase **a él** or **a ella** can be added to the end of the sentence.

  ¿Das el libro a Pablo? Sí, **le** doy el libro **a él**.
  ¿Das el libro a María? Sí, **le** doy el libro **a ella**.

Them can be (1) a direct object or (2) an indirect object. You must determine how the word *them* functions in order to choose the correct pronoun.

- *Do you see the girls? Yes, I see **them**.*

    Function: direct object
    Noun replaced: the girls (**las chicas**)
    Gender in Spanish: feminine

    Therefore, ***them*** = **las**.

  ¿Ves a las chicas? Sí, **las** veo.

- *Do you see the cars? Yes, I see **them**.*

    Function: direct object
    Noun replaced: the cars (**los coches**)
    Gender in Spanish: masculine

    Therefore, ***them*** = **los**.

    ¿Ves los coches? Sí, **los** veo.

- *Did you give the girls the book? Yes, I gave **them** the book.*

    Function: indirect object (I gave the book *to whom*? To them.)
    The book is the direct object.
    Noun replaced: the girls

    Therefore, ***them*** = **les**.

    ¿Dio usted el libro a las chicas? Sí, **les** di el libro.

- *Did you give the boys the book? Yes, I gave **them** the book.*

    Function: indirect object
    Noun replaced: the boys

    Therefore, ***them*** = **les**.

    ¿Dio usted el libro a los chicos? Sí, **les** di el libro.

In order to distinguish **les** which replaces a masculine noun from **les** which replaces a feminine noun, the phrase **a ellos** or **a ellas** can be added to the end of the sentence.

    ¿Dio usted el libro a los chicos? Sí, **les** di el libro **a ellos**.
    ¿Dio usted el libro a las chicas? Sí, **les** di el libro **a ellas**.

Object of Preposition Pronouns

Let's look at the object of preposition pronouns. These pronouns will follow a preposition.

mí	*me*
ti	*you*
él	*him*
ella	*her*
usted	*you*
nosotros/-as	*us*
vosotros/-as	*you*
ellos	
ellas	*them*
ustedes	*you*

*They are leaving **with us**.*
Salen **con nosotros**.

*Michael lives **near me**.*
Miquel vive cerca **de mí**.

In order to use an object of a preposition pronoun in the 3rd person singular or plural you must determine the gender and the number of the noun it replaces.

- *Are you going to the party with John? Yes, I'm going **with him**.*

    Him is the object of the preposition *with*.
    Noun it replaces: John
    Gender and number: masculine singular

    Therefore, ***him*** = él.

    ¿Vas a la fiesta con Juan? Sí, voy **con él**.

- *Do you live near the park? Yes, I live **near it**.*

    It is the object of the preposition *near*.
    Noun it replaces: park **(el parque)**
    Gender and number: masculine singular

    Therefore, ***it*** = él.

    ¿Vives cerca del parque? Sí, vivo **cerca de él**.

- *Are you going to the party with the girls? Yes, I'm going with them.*

  > *Them* is the object of the preposition *with*.
  > Noun it replaces: the girls (**las chicas**)
  > Gender and number: feminine plural
  >
  > Therefore, *them* = **ellas**.

  ¿Vas a la fiesta con las chicas? Sí, voy **con ellas**.

- *Do you live near the mountains? Yes, I live near them.*

  > *Them* is the object of the preposition *near*.
  > Noun it replaces: the mountains (**las montañas**)
  > Gender and number: feminine plural
  >
  > Therefore, *them* = **ellas**.

  ¿Vives cerca de las montañas? Sí, vivo **cerca de ellas**.

Once again we remind you that the types of objects must be identified within the Spanish sentence. Watch the following pitfalls:

1. <u>Object of a preposition in English—Direct object in Spanish</u>

    - *Are you looking at the flowers?*
      Yes, I'm looking at them.

      > object of a preposition pronoun (You are looking *at what*?
      > At the flowers.)

      Function in English: object of a preposition

      However, the Spanish verb **mirar** means *to look at*. The word *at* is contained within the verb; **mirar** is not followed by a preposition. Since there is no preposition, the object is direct.

      ¿Miras las flores?
      Sí, **las** miro.

      > direct object pronoun (¿ Qué miras? Las flores.)

      Function in Spanish: direct object

- *Are you looking for the book?*
  Yes, I'm looking for it.

    object of a preposition pronoun (You are looking *for what*?
    For the book.)

    Function in English: object of a preposition

    However, the Spanish verb **buscar** means *to look for*. The
    word *for* is contained within the verb; **buscar** is not followed
    by a preposition. Since there is no preposition, the object
    is direct.

¿Buscas el libro?
Sí, lo busco.

    direct object pronoun (¿Qué buscas? El libro.)

    Function in Spanish: direct object

2. <u>Subject in English — Indirect Object in Spanish</u>

With some Spanish verbs (**V**) the equivalent of a subject
pronoun (**S**) in English is an indirect object (**IO**) in Spanish.

- *I like the car.*

  S V   DO

  Me gusta el coche.

  IO   V   S

- *He needs a pencil.*

  S   V   DO

  Le falta un lápiz.

  IO   V   S

Let us go over this transformation step by step.

1. Transform the English sentence using an indirect object
   (**IO**) in place of the subject (**S**):

```
/ like the car.    →    The car is pleasing to me.
                        *To me is pleasing the car.

S    V    DO              IO
└_____┘

He needs a pencil. → A pencil is lacking to him.
                     *To him is lacking a pencil.

S    V     DO      IO
└_____────┘
```

2. Express the transformed sentence in Spanish:

*To me is pleasing the car.

Me   gusta   el coche.

*To him is lacking a pencil.

Le   falta   un lápiz.

Here is a list of some of the common verbs which require an indirect object in Spanish where English uses a subject.

doler	*to hurt*
faltar	*to be lacking, to be missing, to need*
gustar	*to be pleasing, to like*
interesar	*to be interesting*
parecer	*to seem*
quedar	*to remain*

Object Pronouns in Summary:

Let's look at the subject and object pronouns side by side so you can see where they differ.

---

*An asterisk before a sentence means that the sentence is ungrammatical. The purpose of including such a sentence is to compare it to the Spanish one.

	Subject	Direct Object	Indirect Object	Object of Preposition
1st pers. sing.	yo	me	me	mí
2nd pers. sing.	tú	te	te	ti
3rd pers. sing.	él	lo	le	él
	ella	la	le	ella
	usted		le	usted
1st pers. pl.	nosotros	nos	nos	nosotros
	nosotras	nos	nos	nosotras
2nd pers. pl.	vosotros	os	os	vosotros
	vosotras	os	os	vosotras
3rd pers. pl.	ellos	los	les	ellos
	ellas	las	les	ellas
	ustedes		les	ustedes

In order to choose the correct pronoun for use in the Spanish sentence follow these steps:

1. Determine the function of the pronoun in Spanish.

   - Is it the subject?
   - Is it the direct object?
   - Is it the indirect object?
   - Is it the object of a preposition?

   In the case of the 3rd person also ask:

   - Is it singular or plural?
   - Is it masculine or feminine?

2. If there are two pronouns, one a direct object and one an indirect object:

   - Proceed as outlined under 1. above for each pronoun individually.
   - Place them in the order as outlined in your Spanish textbook.

< < What is an Interrogative Pronoun? > >

A **pronoun** is a word that stands for one or more nouns. It is a word used instead of a noun. At this point we are going to look at pronouns used to introduce a question; that is, **interrogative pronouns.**

In English: An interrogative pronoun is different if it refers to a person (*who*) or a thing (*what*).

> *What* is on the table?[1]
> *Who* is in the room?

Whom is used when the interrogative pronoun is the object.

> *Whom* are you waiting for?

Otherwise, *who* and *what* do not change.

In Spanish: There are four interrogative pronouns in Spanish: **quién** (*who*), **cuánto** (*how much, how many*), **qué** (*what*) and **cual** (*which*).

1. *Who, whom and whose* = quién or quiénes
   It agrees only in number with the noun it replaces.

   ¿**Quién** viene?　　*Who is coming?*
   　(only one person is coming)

   ¿**Quiénes** vienen?　*Who is coming?*
   　(two or more persons are coming)

   Since there is no English equivalent for **quiénes** both the singular and plural forms translate alike in English. A question with **quién** asks for a singular response:

   ¿Quién viene?　　Juan viene.
   ───────────────
   　　singular subjects

   Who is coming?　　*John is coming.*

---

[1] Do not confuse with "*What* book is on the table?" where *what* is an interrogative adjective. See p. 87.

A question with **quiénes** asks for a plural response:

¿Quiénes vienen?   Juan, Roberto y Miguel vienen.
<u>   </u>
          plural subjects

Who is coming?   John, Robert and Michael are coming.

It will often be necessary to restructure English sentences which contain *who, whom* or *whose* in order to use **quién(es)** correctly in Spanish.

In spoken English we usually separate the interrogative pronoun from its preposition.

Who are you writing *to*?

Who are you going *with*?

Who did you buy the gift *for*?

To express these sentences in Spanish:

- restructure the English sentence so the preposition is followed by the correct interrogative pronoun

Spoken English		Formal English
Who are you writing *to*?	→	*To whom* are you writing?
Who are you leaving *with*?	→	*With whom* are you leaving?
Who did you buy the gift *for*?	→	*For whom* did you buy the gift?

- express the sentences in Spanish

¿**A quién** escribes?
To whom are you writing?

¿**Con quién** sales?
With whom are you leaving?

¿**Para quién** compraste el regalo?
For whom did you buy the gift?

whose = de quién(es)

- restructure the English sentence replacing *whose* with "*of whom*"

Whose car is it?	→	*Of whom* is the car?
Whose house is it?	→	*Of whom* is the house?
Whose books are they?	→	*Of whom* are the books?

- express the sentences in Spanish

¿**De quién** es el coche?
Whose car is it?

¿**De quién** es la casa?
Whose house is it?

¿**De quién** son los libros?
Whose books are they?

2. ***How much* or *how many* = cuánto**
It has four forms to agree in number and gender with the noun it replaces.

- *I have some paper. **How much** do you want?*

Noun replaced: paper (**el papel**)
Gender, number in Spanish: masculine singular

Therefore, *how much* = **cuánto**.

¿**Cuánto** quieres?

- *I have some soup. **How much** do you want?*

Noun replaced: soup (**la sopa**)
Gender, number in Spanish: feminine singular

Therefore, *how much* = **cuánta**.

¿**Cuánta** quieres?

---

*An asterisk before a sentence means that it is ungrammatical.

- *I have some books. **How many** do you want?*

  Noun replaced: books **(los libros)**
  Gender, number in Spanish: masculine plural

  Therefore, *how many* = **cuántos.**

  ¿**Cuántos** quieres?

- *I have some towels. **How many** do you want?*

  Noun replaced: towels **(las toallas)**
  Gender, number in Spanish: feminine plural

  Therefore, *how many* = **cuántas.**

  ¿**Cuántas** quieres?

3. *What* = **qué**
   It has only one form since it is invariable.

   - *__What__ is on the table?*
     ¿**Qué** está sobre la mesa?

   - *__What__ is that?*
     ¿**Qué** es esto?

   NOTE: **Qué** can also be used as an interrogative adjective (see p. 87). As an interrogative adjective **qué** is followed by a noun and means *what* or *which.*

   ¿**Qué** libro tienes?   *__Which__ book do you have?*

4. *__Which one__ or __which ones__* = **cuál**
   It has two forms to agree in number with the noun it replaces.

   - *__Which one__ do you need?*
     ¿**Cuál** necesitas?

   - *__Which ones__ do you need?*
     ¿**Cuáles** necesitas?

   In English the word *one* will not always be expressed.

- *Which of the girls is Spanish?*
  ¿Cuál de las chicas es española?
- *Which of the girls are Spanish?*
  ¿Cuáles de las chicas son españolas?

Which is . . . ? and **Which are . . . ?**   Qué vs. cuál

- ¿ qué + ser . . . ? is used when the expected answer is a definition.

    What is the Nobel Prize?

    > The expected answer is a definition of the Nobel Prize.
    > Therefore, **qué es** is used for *What is . . . ?*

    ¿Qué es el Premio Nobel?

    What are the Panamerican Games?

    > The expected answer is a definition of the Panamerican Games.
    > Therefore, **qué son** is used for *What are . . . ?*

    ¿Qué son los Juegos Panamericanos?

- ¿ cuál(es) + ser . . . ? is used when the expected answer provides one of a number of choices and answers the question which one(s) of many.

    What is your favorite novel?

    > The expected answer will explain which novel of the many that exist is the favorite. Therefore, **cuál es** is used for *What is . . . ?*

    ¿Cuál es su novela favorita?

    What are the countries of Europe?

    > The expected answer will explain which countries of the many in the world are European. Therefore, **cuáles son** is used for *What are . . . ?*

    ¿Cuáles son los países de Europa?

If the "what" of the English question means *which ones*, then use **cuál(es)**.

< < What is a Demonstrative Pronoun? > >

A **demonstrative pronoun** replaces a noun which has been mentioned before. It is called demonstrative because it points out a person or thing. The word demonstrative comes from the same word as *demonstrate*, meaning to point out.

In English: The singular demonstrative pronouns are *this* (*one*) and *that* (*one*); the plural forms are *these* and *those*.

Here are two suitcases. *This one* is big and *that one* is small.

The distinction between *this* and *that* can be used to contrast one object from the other, or to refer to things that are not the same distance away. We generally say *this* for the closer object, and *that* for the one farther away.

In Spanish: The demonstrative pronouns are the same words as the demonstrative adjectives except that all pronoun forms carry a written accent mark in order to distinguish the pronouns from the adjectives. (See **What is a Demonstrative Adjective?**, p. 89.)

- to point out items near the speaker:

    éste, ésta, éstos, éstas (*this, these*)

- to point out items near the person spoken to:

    ése, ésa, ésos, ésas (*that, those*)

- to point out items away from the speaker and the person spoken to:

    aquél, aquélla, aquéllos, aquéllas (*that, those*)

As pronouns these words will replace the demonstrative adjective + noun; they will agree in number and gender with the noun replaced. You will choose the correct form of the demonstrative pronouns in the same way that you choose the correct form of the demonstrative adjectives, that is:

1. Identify the gender and number of the noun replaced.
2. Make the pronoun agree in gender and number with that noun.

- *Give me this book; **this one**.*

  Noun replaced: book (**el libro**)
  Gender, number in Spanish: masc. sing.

  Therefore, ***this one*** = éste.

  Déme este libro; éste.

- *Give me these chairs; **these (ones)**.*

  Noun replaced: chairs (**las sillas**)
  Gender, number in Spanish: fem. pl.

  Therefore, ***these (ones)*** = éstas.

  Déme estas sillas; éstas.

- *Give me that pen near you; **that one**.*

  Noun replaced: pen (**la pluma**)
  Gender, number in Spanish: fem. sing.

  Therefore, ***that one*** = ésa.

  Déme esa pluma; ésa.

- *Give me those books over there; **those (ones)**.*

  Noun replaced: books (**los libros**)
  Gender, number in Spanish: masc. pl.

  Therefore, ***those (ones)*** = aquéllos.

  Déme aquellos libros; **aquéllos**.

Spanish also has three demonstrative pronouns which are used to refer to an idea, item, or previous statement which has no gender or whose gender is not known. These pronouns are therefore said to be neuter in gender and are invariable, that is they never change. They are (1) **esto**, *this (one)*; (2) **eso**, *that (one)*; and (3) **aquello**, *that (one)*.

- *What is **this**?*

  Since it isn't known what "this" is, its gender is also un-known and the neuter form **esto** is used.

  ¿Qué es **esto**?

- *That's not true.*

  That refers to a previous statement and the neuter form **eso** is used.

  Eso *no es verdad.*

- *What is **that** over there?*

  Since it isn't known what "that" is, its gender is also un-known and the neuter form **aquello** is used.

  ¿Qué es **aquello**?

There is another demonstrative pronoun which is being studied separately because it does not follow the same pattern.

In English: The demonstrative pronouns ***the one*** and ***the ones***, unlike *this one* and *that one*, do not point out a specific object, but instead introduce a clause which helps us identify the object by giving additional information about a noun previously mentioned.

- What book are you reading?

  The one (*that*) I bought yesterday.

- Which houses do you prefer?

  The ones that are on Columbus Street.

In Spanish: Forms of the definite article **el, la, los, las** are used as the equivalent of the English demonstrative *the one(s)*. The definite article agrees in number and gender with the noun replaced. *The one* or *the ones* can be used 1. to introduce a clause and 2. to show possession.

1. **the definite article** + *que* is used to introduce a clause. The relative pronoun *that* or **que** in Spanish (see **What is a Relative Pronoun?**, p. 135) which is often omitted in English must be expressed in Spanish. The above sentences in Spanish read as follows:

- ¿Qué libro lees?

  masc. sing.

What book are you reading?

El **que** compré ayer.
masc. sing.

The one (that) I bought yesterday.

- ¿Qué casas prefieres?

  fem. pl.

What houses do you prefer?

Las **que** están en la Calle Colón.
fem. pl.

The ones (that) are on Columbus Street.

2. **the definite article** + *de* is used to show possession.

- *Whose house are you living in?*
  My father's.

  To express "My father's" in Spanish you must first restructure the English phrase.

  My father's → *the one of* my father

  The one depends upon the gender and number of the Spanish noun it replaces: *house* (**la casa**) is fem. sing.

¿En qué casa vives?

    fem. sing.

En la de mi padre.

  fem. sing.

- *Whose pens are these?*
  My brother's.

> My brother's → *the ones of* my brother

The ones depends upon the gender and number of the Spanish noun it replaces: *pens* (**las plumas**) is fem. pl.

¿De quién son las plumas?

       fem. pl.

Son las de mi hermano.

  fem. pl.

Be sure to rework similar English structures before putting them into Spanish.

< < What is a Possessive Pronoun? > >

A **possessive pronoun** is a word which replaces a noun and which also shows who possesses that noun.

Whose house is that?
Mine.

Mine is a pronoun which replaces the noun *house* and which shows who possesses that noun.

In English: Possessive pronouns refer only to the person who possesses, not to the object possessed.

> Example 1. Is that your house? Yes, it is *mine*.
>
> Example 2. Are those your keys? Yes, they are *mine*.

The same possessive pronoun *mine* is used, although the object possessed is singular in Example 1 (*house*) and plural in Example 2 (*keys*).

Here is a list of the English possessive pronouns:

mine	ours
yours	yours
his, hers, its	theirs

The possessive pronoun refers to the person who possesses.

> John's car is blue. *His* is blue.
>
> Mary's car is green. *Hers* is green.

In Spanish: The possessive pronouns have the same forms as the stressed possessive adjectives except that they are normally preceded by the definite article. (See **What is a Possessive Adjective?**, p. 81.) Here is a list of the possessive pronouns used to replace a masculine singular noun.

el mío	*mine*
el tuyo	*yours*
el suyo	*his, hers, yours*
el nuestro	*ours*
el vuestro	*yours*
el suyo	*theirs, yours*

The front part of the possessive pronoun refers to the possessor and the ending agrees with the item or person possessed. The definite article which precedes the possessive pronoun must also agree with the item possessed.

Where are your books? **Mine** *are in the living room.*

> Noun replaced: books **(los libros)**
> Gender, number in Spanish: masculine plural
>
> Therefore, *mine* = **los míos.**

masc. pl. endings

¿Dónde están tus libros? *Los míos* están en la sala.

1st pers. sing. possessor

Compare the agreement of possessive pronouns in English and in Spanish:

		Possessive form in Spanish
English:	Is that ***Paul's*** house? Yes, it's ***his***.	**la suya**
Spanish:	Is that Paul's ***house***? Yes, it's ***his***.	
English:	Is that ***Ann's*** house? Yes, it's ***hers***.	**la suya**
Spanish:	Is that Ann's ***house***? Yes, it's ***hers***.	

The Spanish word for *house* (**la casa**) is feminine singular. Therefore, the possessive pronoun is feminine singular.

English:	Is that ***Paul's*** book? Yes, it's ***his***.	**el suyo**
Spanish:	Is that Paul's ***book***? Yes, it's ***his***.	
English:	Is that ***Ann's*** book? Yes, it's ***hers***.	**el suyo**
Spanish:	Is that Ann's ***book***? Yes, it's ***hers***.	

The Spanish word for *book* (**el libro**) is masculine singular. Therefore, the possessive pronoun is masculine singular.

All the possessive pronouns have a different form for masculine/ feminine and singular/plural. You can find the correct possessive pronoun by following these steps.

1. Determine which definite article will precede the possessive pronoun by establishing the gender and number of the item possessed:

                                                            Definite article

    • if the item possessed is masculine singular
        el libro   *book*   **el**

    • if the item possessed is feminine singular
        la pluma   *pen*   **la**

    • if the item possessed is masculine plural
        los libros   *books*   **los**

    • if the item possessed is feminine plural
        las plumas   *pens*   **las**

2. Indicate the possessor. In Spanish this will be shown by the first letters of the possessive pronouns.

                                        The first letters will be

        mine   **mí-**

        yours   **tuy-**

        his
        hers   **suy-**
        yours

        ours   **nuestr-**

        yours   **vuestr-**

        theirs
        yours   **suy-**

3. Fill in the possessive pronoun so that it will agree in gender and number with the item possessed. Begin by analyzing the gender and number of the item possessed.

- If it is masculine singular, add -o.

  Where is the book? Mine is in the desk.

  Book (**el libro**) is masc. sing.

  ¿Dónde está el libro? **El mío** está en el escritorio.

- If it is feminine singular, add -a.

  Where is the pen? Mine is in the desk.

  Pen (**la pluma**) is fem. sing.

  ¿Dónde está la pluma? **La mía** está en el escritorio.

- If it is masculine plural, add -os.

  Where are the books? Mine are in the desk.

  Books (**los libros**) is masc. pl.

  ¿Dónde están los libros? **Los míos** están en el escritorio.

- If it is feminine plural, add -as.

  Where are the pens? Mine are in the desk.

  Pens (**las plumas**) is fem. pl.

  ¿Dónde están las plumas? **Las mías** están en el escritorio.

Note that these are the regular endings showing number and gender in nouns and adjectives: **-o, -a, -os, -as.**

Let's apply the steps to the following examples.

- *Where are his magazines? **His** are in the desk.*

    1. Selection of definite article.
        The Spanish word for *magazines* (**las revistas**) is
            feminine plural.   **las**
    2. First letters of possessor: *his*   **suy-**
    3. Fill in to agree with item possessed. Add: **-as**

    Completed pronoun   **las suyas**

¿Dónde están sus revistas? **Las suyas** están en el escritorio.

- *Where are her books? **Hers** are in the desk.*

    1. Selection of definite article.
        The Spanish word for *books* (**los libros**) is
            masculine plural.   **los**
    2. First letters of possessor: *hers*   **suy-**
    3. Fill in to agree with item possessed. Add: **-os**

    Completed pronoun   **los suyos**

¿Dónde están sus libros? **Los suyos** están en el escritorio.

- *Where is their book? **Theirs** is in the desk.*

    1. Selection of definite article.
        The Spanish word for *book* (**el libro**) is
            masculine singular.   **el**
    2. First letters of possessor: *theirs*   **suy-**
    3. Fill in to agree with item possessed. Add: **-o**

    Completed pronoun   **el suyo**

¿Dónde está su libro? **El suyo** está en el escritorio.

< < What is a Relative Pronoun? > >

A **relative pronoun** is a word that serves two purposes:

1. As a pronoun it stands for a noun or another pronoun previously mentioned (called its **antecedent**).

   This is the boy *who* broke the window.
   /
   antecedent

2. It introduces a **subordinate clause**; that is, a group of words having a subject and verb separate from the main subject and verb of the sentence.

   This is the boy *who broke the window.*
   └─────────┘ └─────────────────┘
   main clause   subordinate clause

The above subordinate clause is also called a **relative clause** because it starts with a relative pronoun (*who*). The relative clause gives us additional information about the antecedent (*boy*).

In English and in Spanish the relative pronoun used will depend upon the function of the relative pronoun in the relative clause. You must train yourself to go through the following steps.

1. Find the relative clause.
2. Find the relative pronoun.
3. Find the antecedent, the word previously mentioned which the relative pronoun refers to.
4. Determine the function of the relative pronoun in the relative clause.
   - Is it the subject or object?
   - Is it the object of a preposition?
   - Is it a possessive?
5. Select the pronoun according to its antecedent.
   - Is it a thing?
   - Is it a person?

In English: Here are the English relative pronouns.

<u>Subject of the relative clause</u>:

- **who** (if the antecedent is a person)

  This is the student *who* answered.
               /
        antecedent
  Who is the subject of *answered.*

- **which** (if the antecedent is a thing)

  This is the book *which* is so popular.
             /
       antecedent
  Which is the subject of *is.*

- **that** (if the antecedent is a person or a thing)

  This is the student *that* answered.
             /
       antecedent
  That is the subject of *answered.*

  This is the book *that* is so popular.
             /
       antecedent
  That is the subject of *is.*

<u>Object of the relative clause</u>: These pronouns are often omitted in English. We have indicated them in parentheses because they must be expressed in Spanish.

- **whom** (if the antecedent is a person)

  This is the student (*whom*) I saw.
             /   /
      antecedent   subject of relative clause
  Whom is the direct object of *saw.*

- *which* (if the antecedent is a thing)

    This is the book (*which*) I bought.
          antecedent   subject of relative clause
    Which is the direct object of *bought.*

- *that* (if the antecedent is a person or a thing)

    This is the student (*that*) I saw.
          antecedent   subject of relative clause
    That is the direct object of *saw.*

    This is the book (*that*) I read.
          antecedent   subject of relative clause
    That is the direct object of *read.*

These relative pronouns enable you to combine two sentences into one. Look at the following examples:

- Sentence A: That is the boy.
  Sentence B: He broke the window.

You can combine Sentence A and Sentence B by replacing the subject pronoun *he* with the relative pronoun *who.*

That is the boy *who broke the window.*

Who broke the window is the **relative clause.** It does not express a complete thought and it is introduced by a relative pronoun.

Who stands for the noun *boy,* so that *boy* is called the **antecedent** of *who.* Notice that the antecedent stands immediately before the pronoun which gives additional information about it.

Who serves as the subject of the verb *broke* in the relative clause *who broke the window.*

- Sentence A: The Spanish teacher is nice.
  Sentence B: I met her today.

  You can combine Sentence A and Sentence B by replacing the object pronoun *her* with the relative pronoun *whom*.

  The Spanish teacher, *whom I met today*, is nice.

  Whom I met today is the relative clause.

  Whom stands for the noun *teacher*, so that *teacher* is the antecedent. Notice again that the antecedent comes immediately before the relative pronoun.

  Whom serves as the direct object of the relative clause. ("*I*" is the subject.)

- Sentence A: Here is the student.
  Sentence B: I am speaking to him.

  You can combine Sentence A and Sentence B by replacing the indirect object pronoun *to him* with the relative pronoun *to whom*.

  In spoken English, you would combine these two sentences by saying: "Here is the student I am speaking to." This structure will have to be changed.

  Take the preposition *to* at the end of the sentence and place it within the sentence. In order to include *to* within the sentence you will have to add the relative pronoun *whom*.

Here is the student I am speaking *to*.	→	Here is the student *to whom* I am speaking.

Restructuring English sentences which contain a dangling preposition (one where the object does not follow the preposition) will help you identify the relative clause and will give you the correct Spanish word order.

Conversational English	→	Formal English
John is the boy I'm going *with.*	→	John is the boy *with whom* I'm going.
The girls I'm writing *to* live in Madrid.	→	The girls *to whom* I'm writing live in Madrid.
This is the boy I told you *about.*	→	This is the boy *about whom* I told you.

Remember that formal English word order is correct Spanish word order.

In Spanish: There are four main relative pronouns in Spanish: **que, quien(es)**, the forms of **cual** and **cuyo**. Each has its own rules for use and position.

1. *that/which/who/whom* = **que**
   It is invariable; that is, it will not change form to agree with its antecedent. **Que** can be used as a subject or object of a relative clause; it can refer to things or persons.

   A. *that/which/who* as a subject of a relative clause

   - *Here is the phone **that** is not working.*
     *Here is the phone **which** is not working.*
              subject of verb *is working* in the
              clause *that/which is not working.*
     Aquí está el teléfono **que** no funciona.

   - *John is the student **that** answered.*
     *John is the student **who** answered.*
              subject of the verb *answered* in the
              clause *that/who answered.*
     Juan es el estudiante **que** respondió.

B. *that/which/whom* as an object of a relative clause

- *This is the book **that** I bought.*
  *This is the book **which** I bought.*

  > direct object of *bought* in the clause
  > *that/which I bought.*

  Este es el libro **que** compré.

- *John is the boy **that** I admire.*
  *John is the boy **whom** I admire.*

  > direct object of the verb *admire* in the
  > clause *that/whom I admire.*

  Juan es el chico **que** admiro.

2. ***whom*** used as an object of a preposition = **quien or quienes**
    It refers to an antecedent which is a person and agrees with
    the antecedent in number.

    You will often need to restructure the English sentence
    before attempting to put it into Spanish.

- *John is the boy I'm going with.*

John is the boy I'm going *with*.	→	John is the boy *with whom* I'm going.

  > *Whom* is object of preposition *with*.
  > Antecedent is a person (*boy*).

  Juan es el chico **con quien** salgo.

- *The girls I'm writing to live in Madrid.*

The girls I'm writing *to* live in Madrid.	→	The girls *to whom* I'm writing live in Madrid.

  > *Whom* is object of preposition *to*.
  > Antecedent is a person (*girls*).

  Las chicas **a quienes** escribo viven en Madrid.

● *This is the boy I told you about.*

This is the boy I told you *about.*	→	This is the boy *about whom* I told you.

Whom is object of preposition *about*.
Antecedent is a person (*boy*).

Este es el chico **de quien** te hablé.

NOTE: The antecedent of **quien(es)** must be a person. When the object of a preposition refers to a thing then **que** is used as the relative pronoun. Compare the last example above to the following:

This is the book I told you about.

This is the book I told you *about.*	→	This is the book *about which* I told you.

Which is object of preposition *about*.
Antecedent is a thing (*book*).

Este es el libro **de que** te hablé.

3. *that/which/who/whom* in literary Spanish = **cual**
Cual has four forms in order to agree with its antecedents in gender and number: **el cual, la cual, los cuales, las cuales.** Cual can refer to persons or things and can be used as subject or object. Since it changes forms to agree with its antecedent it can often express more clearly the antecedent it is replacing.

English	*John is the student **that** answered.*
Spoken Spanish	Juan es el estudiante **que** respondió.
Literary Spanish	Juan es el estudiante **el cual** respondió.

English	*Mary is the student **that** answered.*
Spoken Spanish	María es la estudiante **que** respondió.
Literary Spanish	María es la estudiante **la cual** respondió.

4. **whose** as a relative possessive[1] = **cuyo**

Cuyo has four forms: **cuyo, cuya, cuyos, cuyas.** The endings agree with the item possessed which will follow the word **cuyo.**

- *The man **whose house** you bought is Mr. Gómez.*
  possessor   item possessed

  > The relative possessive will agree with *house* (**la casa**) which is feminine singular.

  El hombre **cuya casa** compraste es el señor Gómez.
         fem. sing.

- *The lady **whose car** I'm driving is sick.*
  possessor   item possessed

  > The relative possessive will agree with *car* (**el coche**) which is masculine singular.

  La mujer **cuyo coche** manejo está enferma.
        masc. sing.

Let's review the steps for selecting the correct relative pronoun.

1. Find the relative clause; restructure the English clause if necessary.

2. Find the relative pronoun.

3. Find the antecedent.

4. Determine the function of the relative pronoun in Spanish.
   - Is it subject or object? If yes, use
     - A. **que** in conversational Spanish.
     - B. forms of **cual** in literary Spanish.
   - Is it the object of a preposition? If yes, use
     - A. preposition + **que** if the antecedent is a thing.
     - B. preposition + **quien(es)** if the antecedent is a person.

---

[1] **Cuyo** is a relative adjective, not a pronoun but it is included here since it can introduce a relative clause.

- Is it a possessive? If yes, use

  forms of **cuyo** + the item possessed. **Cuyo** will not agree with the antecedent; it agrees with the item possessed.

5. Select the pronoun according to the antecedent (except for **cuyo**).

Let's apply these steps to the following examples.

- *The lady **who** is my neighbor is from France.*
    1. Relative clause: *who is my neighbor*
    2. Relative pronoun: *who*
    3. Antecedent: *the lady* **(la señora)**
    4. Function of *who*: subject
    5. Selection: **que**

La señora **que** es mi vecina es de Francia.

- *Peter and Joe are the boys I was talking **to**.*

Peter and Joe are the boys I was talking *to*.	→	Peter and Joe are the boys *to whom* I was talking.

   1. Relative clause: *to whom I was talking*
   2. Relative pronoun: *whom*
   3. Antecedent: *Peter and Joe*
   4. Function of *whom*: object of preposition *to*
   5. Selection: **quienes**

Pedro y José son los chicos a **quienes** hablaba.

- *Mary is the girl **whose father** is from Greece.*
    1. Relative clause: *whose father is from Greece*
    2. Relative pronoun: *whose*
    3. Antecedent: *girl*
    4. Function of *whose*: possessive
       Item possessed: *father* **(el padre)**
    5. Selection: **cuyo padre**

María es la chica **cuyo padre** es de Grecia.

< < What are Relative Pronouns without Antecedents? > >

The relative pronouns without antecedents are pronouns used to replace a noun which has not been expressed, so that there is no antecedent.

In English: The word **what** meaning *that* which occurs without an antecedent is the common relative pronoun used without an antecedent.

Compare these sentences:

Here is the book (*that*) I read.

antecedent of that: book

Here is *what* I read.

no antecedent

This is *what* happened.

no antecedent

It is easy to see that there is no antecedent because antecedents usually come just before relative pronouns.

In Spanish: The expression **lo que** is the equivalent of the English *what* or *that* without antecedent. **Lo que** is used in conversational Spanish[1] and refers to an idea or previously mentioned statement or concept which has no gender. It can function as a subject or object.

- *What bothers me most is the heat.*

Relative pronoun referring to an idea; it is used as a subject.

Lo que me molesta más es el calor.

- *What you are saying isn't true.*

Relative pronoun referring to a previous statement; it is used as an object.

Lo que dices no es verdad.

---

[1] In literary Spanish **lo cual** is often used instead of **lo que.**

- *I didn't hear **what** he said.*

>> Relative pronoun referring to a previous statement;
>> it is used as an object.

No oí **lo que** dijo.

- *Do you know **what** my daughter did?*

>> Relative pronoun referring to an idea;
>> it is used as an object.

¿Sabes **lo que** hizo mi hija?

< < What are Indefinites and Negatives? > >

Indefinites are words which refer to persons, things or periods of time which are not specific or which are not clearly defined.

In English: Some common indefinites are *someone, anybody, something, some day*. The indefinites are frequently paired with negatives and for convenience these words are often learned as pairs of opposites.

OPPOSITES		
Indefinites		Negatives
someone anyone	≠	no one
somebody anybody	≠	nobody
something anything	≠	nothing
some day any day	≠	never

Is *anyone* coming tonight? *No one.*

Does *anybody* live here? *Nobody.*

Do you have *anything* for me? *Nothing.*

Are you going to Europe *some day*? *Never.*

English sentences use the word ***not*** to become negative. (See **What is a Negative Sentence?**, p. 41.)

I am studying.
I am *not* studying.

In addition, the negative words can also make a statement negative.

No one is coming.
He has *never* seen a movie.

English allows only one negative word in a sentence (or clause). If the word *not* appears, another negative word cannot be used in that same sentence.

*I am *not* studying *nothing*.

This sentence contains a double negative:
not and *nothing*.
It is incorrect English.

The indefinite word which is the opposite of the negative word is used in sentences containing *not*.

I am *not* studying *anything*.

---

*An asterisk before a sentence means that the sentence is ungrammatical. The purpose of including such a sentence is to compare it to the Spanish one.

Here is another example.

I have *nothing*.	*Nothing* is the one negative word.
I do *not* have *anything*.	The sentence contains *not*; therefore, the word *anything* is substituted for *nothing*.
*I do *not* have *nothing*.	This sentence contains a double negative—*not* and *nothing*—and is incorrect English.

In Spanish: As in English, the indefinites and negatives exist as pairs of opposites.

Indefinites		Negatives	
something *anything* *everything*	algo todo	nada	*nothing*
some, any *several* *someone*	algún alguno	ningún ninguno	*no, none* *not any*
someone/somebody *anyone/anybody* *everyone/everybody*	alguien todos	nadie	*no one,* *nobody*
some day *always* *sometimes*	algún día siempre a veces	nunca jamás	*never* *not ever*
also, too	también	tampoco	*not ... either*
either, or	o	ni	*neither* *neither, nor*
either ... or	o ... o	ni ... ni	*neither ... nor*

Notice that most indefinites begin with the letters **alg-** and the negatives begin with **n-**.

---

*An asterisk before a sentence means that the sentence is ungrammatical. The purpose of including such a sentence is to compare it to a correct sentence.

The indefinites and negatives belong to several parts of speech.

algo	nada	Pronouns; they do not change form.
alguien	nadie	Pronouns; they do not change form.
alguno	ninguno	Adjectives or pronouns, they have four forms to agree in gender and number with the nouns they modify or replace.
algún día	nunca	Adverbs; they do not change form.
también	tampoco	Adverbs; they do not change form.

Contrary to English, the indefinites cannot appear in a negative Spanish sentence. If the Spanish sentence contains **no** meaning *not* an indefinite cannot be used in that same sentence (or clause). A negative is used in place of the indefinite.

English: I do ***not*** have ***anything***.
  not indefinite word

Spanish: **No** tengo **nada**.
  not negative word (*nothing*)

English:	*not* + **indefinite word**
Spanish:	*no* + **negative word**

In order to use the indefinites and negatives correctly in Spanish it will often be necessary to re-word the English sentence so that *not* will be followed by a negative word, the opposite of the English indefinite.

I do *not* see *anybody*. → *I do *not* see *nobody*.

Then express in Spanish.

No veo a **nadie**.

---

*An asterisk before a sentence means that the sentence is ungrammatical. The purpose of including such a sentence is to compare it to the Spanish one.

Let's look at some other examples.

- *I do **not** want to eat **anything**.*

1.	Locate the indefinite:	anything
2.	Decide what the opposite of the English indefinite is:	anything → nothing
3.	Transform the English sentence using a double negative:	*I do *not* want to eat *nothing.*
4.	Put the sentence into Spanish.	

  No quiero comer **nada**.

- *I don't (do **not**) have **any** book.*

1.	Locate the indefinite:	any
2.	Decide what the opposite of the English indefinite is:	any → no
3.	Transform the English sentence using a double negative:	*I do*n't* have *no* book.
4.	Put the sentence into Spanish.	

  No tengo **ningún** libro.

---

*An asterisk before a sentence means that the sentence is ungrammatical. The purpose of including such a sentence is to compare it to the Spanish one.

< < Index > >